MW00452626

BOSS
BRAIN

Unlock Your Entrepreneurial Instincts

TRA WILLIAMS

Mechanicsburg, PA USA

Published by Sunbury Press, Inc.
Mechanicsburg, PA USA

www.sunburypress.com

For information about special discounts for bulk purchases, please contact Sunbury Press Orders Dept. at (855) 338-8359 or orders@sunburypress.com.

To request one of our authors for speaking engagements or book signings, please contact Sunbury Press Publicity Dept. at publicity@sunburypress.com.

FIRST SUNBURY PRESS EDITION: August 2021

Set in Adobe Garamond | Interior design by Crystal Devine | Cover by Lawrence Knorr | Illustrations by James Culver | Edited by Rea Frey, Joe Tower, and Lawrence Knorr.

Publisher's Cataloging-in-Publication Data
Names: Williams, Tra, author.
Title: Boss brain : unlock your entrepreneurial instincts / Tra Williams.
Description: First hard cover edition. | Mechanicsburg, PA : Sunbury Press, 2021.
Summary : Based on proven scientific research, Boss Brain masterfully traces the spirit and psychology of entrepreneurship through a sweeping arc of history. Using stories that skip across time—from the height of the Roman Empire to the moon landing—it empowers aspiring entrepreneurs with a detailed system to overcome the fear of uncertainty, escape the cage of mediocrity, and never be an employee again.
Identifiers: ISBN : 978-1-62006-871-7 (Hard cover).
Subjects: BUSINESS & ECONOMICS / Entrepreneurship | SELF-HELP / Personal Growth / Success | SELF-HELP / Personal Growth / Happiness.

Product of the United States of America
0 1 1 2 3 5 8 13 21 34 55

Continue the Enlightenment!

CONTENTS

FOREWORD

You have a problem. Yes, you. I know that's an inflammatory way to start a book, but it's the truth. Your problem is not that you've done something wrong intentionally; it's that you don't always realize the ways in which you are on autopilot. It's not that you're living a bad life. It's more that life is living you. The good news is that you're holding a book that can help you the way that it has helped me.

The purpose of *Boss Brain* is to shine a light into some of the forgotten corners of your life, bringing you face-to-face with the innate and sometimes unconscious things you do to sabotage yourself. You may not be aware of any intentional self-sabotage, of course, which speaks to the true power of the book. It is revolutionary precisely because the thoughts and behaviors targeted are silent and insidious. By illuminating these reflexive errors in thinking and behaving, you'll be better equipped to live life on purpose; an incredible goal achievable only by those willing to do the sometimes painful introspecting that *Boss Brain* will bring about.

You will become aware of how you have sold yourself short because doing so has become second nature. Within, you will learn that your mind is wired to protect the status quo while your heart is wired for greatness. Your brain tells lies that keep you fed and safe, but they also make you soft and sad. Unless you learn to recognize and break free of the deep grooves of banality that society has tread for you, you will always find your life lacking in some important, if ineffable, way. If you've ever had the thought, "Something is missing, and I can't quite put my finger on it," *Boss Brain* has both the diagnosis and the cure for what ails you.

To begin to understand the problem that I mentioned at the outset, consider something you've always wanted to do but that you've put off for whatever reason. Maybe that something is having a child. Maybe it's starting a business. Or perhaps it's writing a book, getting serious with a romantic partner, or any number of other aspirations you've yet to reach. Let's say for discussion's sake that the thing you are considering is starting a business. You ask yourself:

"Should I start a business?"

Ostensibly, you should make a T-chart, list the pros and cons, and then decide. Easy enough, right? Well, let's examine how you go about dissecting this question. You do your best to dispassionately weigh the pros and perils. But, if you're like most folks, there is a flaw in the system.

Drawing on his background in evolutionary psychology, James Friedrich has concluded that as we evaluate important decisions in our life, our primary aim is to avoid the costliest errors. That is, we make decisions that make us *not unhappy* rather than *blissful*. We want to be "not broke" more than we want to live abundantly. A lifetime of this calculus leaves us unfulfilled and, in many cases, unable to say exactly why.

In the U.S. and Western Europe, most people have the base of Maslow's pyramid met—they have adequate food, water, sleep, and safety. In the face of so much abundance, why is it that Western society is increasingly beset by "deaths of despair" like suicide and drug overdoses? Having now met these basic needs, they are left to wrangle with more metaphysical concerns such as belonging and self-actualization. No writer has expressed this existential struggle more succinctly and beautifully than Chuck Palahniuk, who said, through his character Tyler Durden, "We're the middle children of history, man. No purpose or place. We have no Great War. No Great Depression. Our great war is a spiritual war. Our great depression is our lives."

We are left only with a brain and a decision-making modality that is ill-suited for our modern milieu. We are programmed to choose safety, even at the expense of joy, in an environment where safety abounds, and joy is hard to find. Numerous studies have shown that people are twice as upset about a loss as they are pleased about a gain. Unless we learn to train our brains to evaluate risk and reward on a more even keel, we will remain trapped in a life of risk-aversion that keeps us from taking the very risks that might make us happy.

The power of the book that you hold in your hand is that it will awaken you to this reality in new and surprising ways from which there is no returning. You will be brought to a crossroads where you are forced to reckon with your own subtle self-deception and choose either to start living on purpose or to accept that you have created your own cage of discontent.

If you choose to continue reading, and I hope that you will, you will be brought face-to-face with some uncomfortable truths. You will squirm. You will feel implicated. You will recognize unintentional missteps in yourself that have hurt you in the past. You may even get angry and wish you could go back to living life with blinders on. If you're not prepared for this, maybe you should put this book down and pick up something with a glossy cover and big letters on the front. Better yet, go watch TV.

But if you are ready to sit with that discomfort on the way to a better-vetted and more fulfilling life, read on because what follows promises to be as meaningful as it is hard to hear.

As Viktor Frankl said so beautifully, "Between stimulus and response, there is a space. In that space is our power to choose our response. In our response lies our growth and freedom." As you read this book, you will find yourself in the very space that Frankl spoke of and emerge with tools and techniques for bringing about that growth and freedom.

Life is funny—absurd even, according to existential philosophers like Frankl. We spend our lives wringing our hands about grownup monsters in the closet—wild animals, serial killers, killer bees, and the like—when in actuality, the greatest risks to our well-being are the self-limiting voices in our heads. Tra Williams has heard those voices, learned to overcome them, and with this book, has fashioned a shield to protect you from the monsters of your own undoing.

Daniel Crosby, PhD

PREFACE

"BECAUSE IN THE END, YOU WON'T REMEMBER THE
TIME YOU SPENT WORKING IN THE OFFICE OR MOWING
YOUR LAWN. CLIMB THAT GODDAMN MOUNTAIN."
—JACK KEROUAC

Aspiring entrepreneurs are instinctively driven to be the master of their own fate and to explore the limits of their potential. But simultaneously, most of them hear a second and different internal dialogue. They are often conflicted, like a voice in their head is holding them back. When discussing opportunity, would-be entrepreneurs are optimistic, engaged, and filled with confidence. However, when the conversation turns to entrepreneurship's inherent uncertainty, they often become more reserved and less sure of themselves. It's like two different people are in their heads. The optimistic voice tells them all the reasons they should start their own business. But the other voice, the one that fears uncertainty, tells them all the reasons they should remain someone else's employee.

In the past century, we have allowed one of those voices to conquer the other. We have buried our innate, entrepreneurial instincts beneath a mountain of lies. Some lies we are told; some lies we tell others. But the worst lies are the ones we tell ourselves. As a result, aspiring entrepreneurs now feel like they're meant for something more but are stuck where they are.

As vice president and president of two international franchise brands, I have worked with thousands of entrepreneurs. In that time, I have personally witnessed the conflict between our instinctive optimism and our fear of uncertainty. Some eagerly embrace one, while its counterpart overcomes others.

I have heard these two voices myself, and it was not a pleasant experience.

Twice in the past decade, I found myself unemployed due to mergers and acquisitions. The uncertainty of my future at that time made me feel incredibly conflicted. One day I would be determined to start my own business and never again give someone else control over my life. The next day I would frantically search the Internet for jobs. My instincts were telling me to be my own boss, but my fear of uncertainty was telling me I should just find another job.

I realized then that entrepreneurship is about so much more than business ownership. It is about listening to our instincts and not being paralyzed by the fear of uncertainty.

Humans have always been driven by the instinct to explore the limits of their potential. Throughout history, we have expanded our frontiers, always pushing past the known into the unknown. Long before money was invented, our entrepreneurial instincts inspired us to undertake seemingly impossible risks. Time and again, we have conquered our fear of uncertainty, even without knowing the full extent of the potential rewards. In this sense, entrepreneurship isn't just an action we take. It is a way of thinking—a mindset. It's not just a method of earning. It is a way of life.

Our Creator gave us an inner calling to explore the limits of our potential. In fact, the word *entrepreneur* comes from an ancient Sanskrit phrase that means *inner calling*. Then and now, some of us listen to that calling and follow it. Others do not. That's because, in her eminent wisdom, Mother Nature balanced our adventurous impulses with an opposing force, the second voice in our head. Together, they are our yin and yang, our fire and ice. As one pushes, the other pulls. While one inspires action, the other advises restraint.

Our success as a species required that some stay behind while others sailed beyond the horizon. It was Mother Nature's method of ensuring that we would learn from trial and error; her little way of making sure that each generation would be smarter and more capable than the last.

She did this to protect us from being overly optimistic, not to bind us to our need for certainty. But that is exactly what has happened. The ice of uncertainty has smothered the fire of our optimism.

Twelve thousand years ago, the struggle between our optimism and our need for certainty created a tipping point. It was an innocuous transition that, at first, shifted us ever so slightly toward the cage in which we now find ourselves. At the time, it probably felt subtle. But as centuries passed, it has proven to be a watershed event, one that has cascaded unintended consequences on the generations that followed. We forgot how to live in harmony with our instincts. We forgot how to do what we had always done, how to be what we really are. We developed insecurities and placated them with egotistical self-deceptions. Eventually, the magnitude of our struggle manifested irrational fears. At first, we began to dread what lay beyond the flickering glow of the campfire. Then, we fretted over the uncertainty of life without daily predictability. And finally, we ceded all control to the fear of being singularly accountable for our own fate.

We traded our potential for predictable adequacy. We sold our freedom for twenty-six paychecks a year.

Most entrepreneurship-focused, how-to books start at the point where a business is conceptualized or created. This is not that book. In fact, the last chapter of this book ends at the point where your business begins. That's because the pages that follow don't explain how to do what you've never done. Instead, they reveal how to break free from all the lies of the modern world and once again be what you really are. As the following pages will reveal, you were born with all the instincts and cunning required for entrepreneurship. And deep down inside, you already know this to be true.

So, instead of touting the guiding principles depicted within these pages as somehow groundbreaking or revelatory, I will offer this stark reminder: Mother Nature is brutal. She has no tolerance for excuses. She has wisely and sometimes cruelly honed our instincts into a weapon, one that far exceeds the power of fangs and claws. We need only to listen to her voice and ignore all others, even our own.

This book is not the solution to all your problems. It is not a silver bullet that will slay your inner demons, nor is it a sword of power to wield as you carve your way out of traditional employment. Instead, this book is more like a shield. Like all shields, it will protect you from harm as you wade into battle. But unlike most shields, this book wasn't written to protect you from your enemies.

This book was written to protect you from yourself.

Boss Brain traces the spirit and psychology of entrepreneurship through a sweeping arc of history beginning 12,000 years ago when our species put down spears and picked up shovels. With stories that skip across time—from the height of the Roman Empire, through medieval times, past the age of enlightenment, all the way to the Renaissance, the birth of America, and the moon landing—*Boss Brain* reveals why the human drive to explore the limits of our potential will always be our defining characteristic. Unlike every other species on this planet, we want our lives to be more and mean more. This is what sets us apart—the hallmark of our kind. It is neither technology, art, literature, nor science but the desire to build a legacy that defines us as human.

The pages that follow will empower you to build your own legacy using a proven system that unlocks your entrepreneurial instincts so that you can leave traditional employment forever—that's the *real* American Dream. If you know that you were meant to be the master of your own fate, and if you are willing to accept sole responsibility for making that vision a reality, then join me on this journey to entrepreneurship.

BOSS BRAIN SPONSORS

The following organizations strongly support startups, small businesses, and the real American Dream. Visit them online today and learn more about how they can help you unleash your entrepreneurial spirit.

The Winter Haven Chamber of Commerce is committed to advancing commerce and community by serving, representing, and enhancing business growth throughout Central Florida. We believe that equipping more people to become entrepreneurs accelerates both individual opportunity and community prosperity. Learn more at WinterHavenChamber.com.

Simple Again is the natural place to start your own juice bar business. We've launched thousands of successful juice bars in the past 20 years, and each was branded to fit our customer's vision. We are your one-stop-shop juice bar partner. Start your new juice bar business today at www.SimpleAgain.com.

swiig

swiig™ provides natural and organic smoothie ingredients for your home or business. Our mission is to deliver only ingredients with certified sources. We never allow GMOs or artificial junk. Our ingredients provide clean nutrition from clean sources. swiig™ – stuff with infinite goodness! Find your goodness at www.swiig.com.

SPECIAL THANKS

Carousel's Soft Serve Icery – Carousels.com

Antwerp Diamonds of Buckhead and Roswell –
    AntwerpDiamondStore.com

Spoiled Rotten Photography — SpoiledRottenPhotography.com

FleetForce Truck Driving School — DriveFleetForce.com

Hueman People Solutions — Hueman.com

Patterson Financial — PFFirm.com

Lakeview Center — eLakeviewCenter.org

Constant Mountain — ConstantMountain.com

SCORE SC Lowcountry — SCLowcountry.score.org

NGP Financial Planning— NGPFinancial.com

Writeway — Writewayco.com

Melissa W. Richardson

INTRODUCTION

"THERE WAS ABOUT HIM A SUGGESTION OF LURKING
FEROCITY, AS THOUGH THE WILD STILL LINGERED IN
HIM AND THE WOLF IN HIM MERELY SLEPT."
—JACK LONDON, *WHITE FANG*

Your brain is ancient. For 200,000 years, Mother Nature has molded it through natural selection. In its most primitive parts, she added instincts, intuition, and, most importantly, the ability to envision the future. While other animals lived in the moment and focused only on survival, Mother Nature gave early humans the power to visualize the future and the intrinsic motivation to make that vision a reality. The most primitive part of your brain, the part that carried humans out of the caves of Africa to every corner of the globe, still speaks to you today. It is your Boss Brain.

Your Boss Brain is the primitive hardware that houses the four primary instincts that humans needed to flourish for nearly 200,000 years. Through epochs of time, it prospered without ego or identity. It evolved in a world that offered no certainty. Everything was a gamble. Survival required self-reliance and intrinsic motivation. Each day the Boss Brain traded time, energy, and resources for sustenance, longevity, and legacy—just like a modern entrepreneur.

Of course, early man was not yet the CEO of the planet; humans weren't even at the top of the food chain. Our ancestors conquered the world when there were no state-sponsored expeditions or politically motivated land grabs. Those who reached previously unknown shores didn't plant a flag and claim the land for some king or queen. There *were* no kings or queens. The small bands of humans that spread across and populated the planet did so without centralized governments or standing armies. Money didn't motivate them because money didn't exist. A more fundamental human instinct drove them—the instinct to explore the limits of their potential and for that exploration to be their legacy.

If survival was the only motivation, man would have never left the caves. If procreation was the only motivation, man would have never climbed mountains. Therefore, sustenance and longevity were only essential because they contributed to the real goal: legacy.

It is not meaning or purpose but legacy that drives the entrepreneur. The opportunity to achieve, to build something that will last long after you are gone, and to be remembered for it. Just like your ancestors, your Boss Brain longs for the freedom to build a legacy. The hunger for this freedom will never die. It is deep-seated and an essential part of what makes you human.

Society is full of opportunities to build a legacy. It is also full of expectations that didn't exist when your Boss Brain evolved. It took 195,000 years for man to go from throwing rocks to swinging swords. It took 3000 years to go from swords to cannons, and just 700 years to go from cannons to nuclear bombs. Until recently, you could be dropped into almost any point in human history thousands of years apart and notice little difference. Today, a few decades have reshaped humanity.

Our brains were not designed to manage the intricacies of modern society with all its rules, standards, customs, and expectations. The pressure you feel to meet those expectations traps you somewhere between what you are and who you are told you have to be. As a result, you feel like you're meant for something more but are stuck where you are. Your instincts tell you to do one thing while the world tells you to do the opposite.

From an evolutionary perspective, the social complexities that you must navigate each day are shockingly new compared to the antiquity of your brain. A few thousand years might sound like a long time, but the modern world in which you live is in its infancy. For example, the structure of contemporary employment has existed for about .06% of the time since the human brain emerged. If you compressed all of humanity into 60 seconds, the mantra of "go to school, get a job, and buy a house" would comprise less than *four one-hundredths* of a second.

Mother Nature simply did not wire us to execute a mindless routine each day. We were not designed to be cogs in the wheels of society. We most certainly were not meant to have our lives dictated to us by our jobs. For 99.94% of our time on earth, we thrived in the freedom to explore our potential in whatever way we chose.

However, your ancient brain now exists in a strange place that conflicts with its internal wiring. Every day, your brain is inundated with demands. The outside world tells you where to go, what to do, when to do it, how to dress, how to talk, and how to act. While your instincts speak to you from the inside, societal expectations scream at you from the outside—it's like having two voices battling inside your head.

So, in a way, you have two brains: your Boss Brain and your modern brain.

Your Boss Brain came first. It is driven by the need to explore the limits of its potential. As Mother Nature honed its wiring, she selected complacency, self-doubt, and dependence for extinction. The unforgiving laws of natural selection whittled at our DNA until our brains held everything we needed to succeed. In the end, she wired us with four primary instincts: belief, accountability, focus, and creativity. Once they were set in motion, man's epic rise became inevitable.

Despite its ambitious nature, your Boss Brain is not domineering or bossy. It does not seek authority over others. It seeks only to maximize its freedom and build the best life possible. Modern entrepreneurs are no different. They want to maximize the freedoms they are afforded and realize all that is within the limits of their capabilities. As an employee, you can only prove that you are capable of doing what the job requires. The work might be challenging, but rarely does an employer require employees to explore the limits of all that is within their physical and mental capacity. A person cannot know their capabilities without testing themselves.

None of your ancestors failed that test. Your DNA carries the genes of only those who successfully broke away from larger groups and built a better life. How do I know this? Because you are alive! You are part of a successful lineage of Boss Brains who proved their abilities. Their voices whisper to you every time rush hour traffic makes you miss your daughter's soccer game or your vacation request gets denied. They say, "This is not what you are. You are capable of so much more."

Your Boss Brain evolved before society peddled the idea that we must compete against each other as we climb the ladder within corporate hierarchies. Your ancestors would simply leave an overly competitive or oppressive situation and rely on themselves. They passed that inherent desire for independence on to you. Mother Nature's slow and methodical process selected your Boss Brain for survival. You were born with all the instincts that made humans successful. In other words, you are wired for success. All the primal motivations that emanate from within your brain are there for a reason. Had any of them been detrimental to your survival, they would not have been chosen by natural selection.

Next came your modern brain. It isn't a separate structure; it is the complex software that society loaded onto your ancient hardware about twelve thousand years ago. Your modern brain does everything it can to suppress the four primary instincts of the Boss Brain because it craves certainty—and the chaos of contemporary society only multiplies this desire. Your modern brain is driven by the fear of losing anything reliable and predictable.

The modern brain is also obsessed with itself. It constantly ruminates on who it is and how others perceive it. It lives in a world that rewards conformity and assimilation. As modern society hones and refines its expectations, individualism and independence are being selected for social extinction.

Most everyone who considers leaving their job and starting a business feels some level of anxiety over the implications. That inner turmoil and the stress that ensues is the struggle between your Boss Brain and your modern brain. Your Boss Brain feels caged by employment while your modern brain fears the uncertainty of entrepreneurship. Inevitably, that turmoil becomes frustration and angst because you feel trapped between what you really are and who you are told you have to be.

To compensate for feeling trapped, the modern brain creates excuses and self-deceptions. It tells you lies, and you believe them because you want to think the best of yourself. In this way, each person is complicit in the destruction of their dreams. In the end, the excuses that you make to protect your self-perception become the chains that bind you from taking action.

Fortunately, Mother Nature devised a simple and elegant mental framework to overcome this psychological pitfall. Coincidentally, it is the same framework that ensured humanity would do more than just survive; we would thrive. Mother Nature wove four primary entrepreneurial instincts into our DNA. In this book, they are called Primary Instincts because they were the foundation of our original ascent. They were the cornerstones of the psychological puzzle that empowered us to overcome every challenge we faced throughout history. They are the baseline of our existence that we automatically default to when left to fend for ourselves.

The four Primary Instincts of your Boss Brain are Belief, Accountability, Focus, and Creativity. All four are interdependent. Together, they flow in a cycle where each perpetuates the next. They might not sound like much individually, but as the pages that follow will show, when all four are nurtured and used in tandem, you become unstoppable. However, if just one of the Primary Instincts of your Boss Brain is suppressed by your modern brain, the cycle stops flowing. At that point, the other three are rendered useless. That is the sinister and invisible power of self-deception. One small lie can derail your entire entrepreneurial effort.

Accordingly, this book is divided into four parts—four categories of lies that suppress the four Primary Instincts. Each part is followed by key points and questions to ask yourself.

PART I: THE LIES THAT WE TELL EACH OTHER

We are all given conflicting messages from the time we can talk. We encourage each other to be authentic and follow our dreams. At the same time, we tell each other to go to school and get a good job. This section outlines the origins of the inner conflict between entrepreneurship and employment.

PART II: THE LIES THAT WE TELL OURSELVES

As we age, we develop defense mechanisms to protect our self-perception. We claim to be victims of circumstance and pretend that business ownership just wasn't meant to be. This section reveals why the lies we tell ourselves are always the most deceiving.

PART III: THE LIES THAT WE TELL OTHERS

After a lifetime of self-deceit, we must make excuses for our inaction. Whether it's time, money, or fate, the excuses we make become the chains that bind us. This section brings clarity out of chaos.

PART IV: THE LIES WE ARE TOLD

Collectively, we shun anyone who dares to walk a non-traditional path. In doing so, we hinder innovation and our advancement. This section outlines the importance of diversity in our thoughts and actions.

PART V: UNLEASHING YOUR BOSS BRAIN

The Four Primary Instincts of the Boss Brain need to be set in motion. Part V is more than a practical application of what you have learned. It is also an ignition switch that starts the flow of your entrepreneurial instincts.

Unlike rules and guidelines, the four Primary Instincts of the Boss Brain are immutable. They are the pillars of humanity. They guided us out of our caves and to every corner of the globe, and they can now guide you out of employment and into entrepreneurship.

C H A P T E R   1

GET A GOOD JOB

"RISK IS THE TARIFF PAID TO LEAVE THE SHORES
OF PREDICTABLE MISERY."
—AMAR LAVANI, CEO STANDARD HOTELS

Right now, 100 million Americans want to quit their jobs and start their own businesses. But while 70% of the American workforce *wants* to be self-employed, less than 7% *is*. Despite all the current talk about the gig economy, the widening gap between entrepreneurship and employment in America is the largest in history. Each year, more and more Americans want to start their own business. Yet each year, fewer and fewer do.

With very few exceptions, self-employment rates in America have decreased every year since the baby boom. Just twenty-five years ago, entrepreneurs made up more than 12% of the workforce. Today, it is little more than half that. And self-employment rates aren't just low by American standards. They now rank among the lowest of any country in the world. But the most striking aspect of the entrepreneurship gap is that it crosses all races, genders, education levels, and socio-economic barriers.

For most, the American Dream will always be just a dream.

Fortunately, even though business creation continues to trend downward, Americans haven't lost their infamous entrepreneurial spirit.

Millennial and Gen Z workers have strong self-employment inclinations. As they entered the workforce, the percentage of would-be entrepreneurs in America has trended upward and now ranks third in the world behind Poland and Portugal.[1] Russia, Denmark, and Norway are at the bottom of the entrepreneurial spirit list—only about 30% of their citizens want to be self-employed. Despite their apparent lack of entrepreneurial spirit, all three currently boast higher levels of actual entrepreneurship than the United States.[2]

Many would-be entrepreneurs blame their inaction on a lack of resources. But America has the most extensive system for small business funding and support in the world. The U.S.A. has more small business loan programs, grants, scholarships, educational courses, and business development organizations than the rest of the world combined. In fact, many countries with much higher levels of self-employment offer just a fraction of the support provided in America.

The problem is not a lack of desire or opportunity.

Economists and politicians love to point at one statistic or another and blame some aspect of society for the reduction in startups. But the only thing that could stop 100 million Americans from doing what they want is 100 million Americans. Our entrepreneurial instincts are losing a battle against a tenacious and invisible enemy: ourselves. More and more, we are not *choosing* to explore the limits of our potential. Instead, we are choosing predictable misery over the misery of uncertainty.

OPTIMISM AND ENTREPRENEURSHIP

Humans instinctively avoid taking steps that we expect will yield a negative result. When you do something, you do it because you think good outcomes will follow. Whether it's buying a house, selling a home, or changing jobs, you do it because you believe that action will produce a positive effect. Today we call it optimism—the belief that events in the future will be better than the present and the past.

Every action, no matter how small, was born of optimism. Even small, seemingly inconsequential decisions are optimistic. You eat healthy

---

1. David Blanchflower, "Measuring Latent Entrepreneurship Across Nations," Department of Economics, Dartmouth College and NBER, USA, 2000.
2. OECD (2020), Self-employment rate (indicator). doi: 10.1787/fb58715e-en.

because you believe that doing so will make you feel and look better. You choose your route to work because you believe it is better or faster than the others. You look at the weather before getting dressed because dressing appropriately will make your day better. Better and better and better. We are wired to seek opportunities to improve our circumstances and our lives.

Imagine the first humans ever to build a raft and sail beyond the horizon. They had no idea if other lands even existed. But they weren't just optimistic, they also genuinely believed in their ability to figure out how to handle whatever challenges arose. With limited food and water, death was the consequence of being wrong. That is the power of having an optimistic vision of the future and trust in your own abilities. That is the power of your Boss Brain.

When early humans emerged on the savannas of Africa, they were just another animal attempting to find their place in the food chain. Their cunning took them across continents and oceans. However, it was not math or the power of deduction that motivated them to explore. It was the capacity to envision a better life somewhere other than where they were. And in that life, they would flourish, thrive, and reproduce without worry or concern.

Psychologists initially rejected the idea that humans are instinctively optimistic. But Tali Sharot, author of *The Optimism Bias*, has proven that humans are inherently optimistic. Psychologists have now embraced the critical role optimism played in human development. The ability to envision a better future in a different place or time was crucial. Sharot noted that the bias "protects and inspires us: it keeps us moving . . . without optimism, our ancestors might never have ventured far from their tribes, and we might all be cave dwellers, still huddled together and dreaming of light and heat." And without optimism, we would all be employees.

Studies have even isolated a gene within your DNA that appears to be responsible for your lofty expectations. It was passed to you by your ancestors, who were very likely to be optimistic. How do we know? A study from the Boston University of Medicine recently proved it. They found that optimistic women have a whopping 50% better chance of reaching the age of 85, and men have a 70% better chance of living longer than their pessimistic brothers. These aren't incremental advantages. The effect optimism has on longevity is monumental. Many studies have verified this, showing a direct relationship between optimism and significantly increased longevity even after adjusting for behavioral factors.[3]

Longer lives provide more opportunities to have kids and build support networks through multi-generational communities. The pessimists who lived shorter lives were not afforded those opportunities and, therefore, were less likely to pass on their pessimistic genes.[4] As its effect compounded over time, optimism served as a fundamental element in the rise of humanity.

A vast amount of research also shows that within the context of entrepreneurship, optimists actually enjoy experiencing various forms of adversity. They are motivated by challenges and find difficult situations as an opportunity to explore their potential.[5] Optimists typically rise to face the problems that life presents to them, persisting and remaining engaged in pursuing their goals.[6] Conversely, pessimists lack tenacity and persistence and quickly give up when faced with adversity.[7]

Without the unique ability to envision a better future, humans would have quickly given up and settled for a compromised existence. Our optimism inspired action 100,000 years ago, just as it inspires entrepreneurs today. Without optimism, there is no inner calling, no deep-seated desire to build the best life possible. Despite our past negative experiences, we dream of the future as a better place, and we are genetically hardwired to seek it out.

CERTAINTY AND EMPLOYMENT

One of the most well-established tenets of psychology is the brain's bias toward consistency and predictability. The mind wants its expectations

3. Lewina O. Lee, et al, "Optimism is associated with exceptional longevity in 2 epidemiologic cohorts of men and women," *Proc Natl Acad Sci USA*, 2019; 116:18357-18362.

4. Hilary A. Tindle, et al, "Optimism, cynical hostility, and incident coronary heart disease and mortality in the Women's Health Initiative," *Circulation*, 2009;120:656–662.

5. Gideon D. Markman, et al, "Are perseverance and self-efficacy costless? Assessing entrepreneurs' regretful thinking," *Journal of Organisational Behaviour*, Vol.26 No.1, pp.1-19.

6. C. S. Carver and M. Scheier, "Optimism" In S. J. Lopez, and Snyder, C. R. (Ed.), *Positive Psychological Assessment: A Handbook of Models and Measures*, 2003.

7. Sibin Wu, et al, "'Need for achievement, business goals, and entrepreneurial persistence," *Management Research News*, Vol. 30 No. 12, pp. 928-941.

met. It needs consistent outcomes above all else and to maintain a continuum of beliefs, attitudes, and behaviors. Predictable results may require more work and offer fewer rewards, but they also require less thought. When predictable options are available, certainty overcomes quality—predictability overcomes optimism.

The Boss Brain of ancient man enjoyed predictability but on a massive scale. The cycles of the seasons and migrations of animals were predictable. Each day brought new challenges and lacked the monotony of the modern world because early man did not attempt to tame his environment.

We dream of the future as a better place, and we are genetically hardwired to seek it out.

For employees, modern life doesn't flow within a natural order. Society revolves around the workday, and the workday doesn't change with the seasons. Without an overarching seasonal strategy, annual migrations are now compressed into daily routines. Predictability is maintained by the minute at a micro-level. Our lives are governed by the clock, not the calendar.

The simplest and quickest way to achieve minute-by-minute consistency is to accept a role from within the options that society has made readily available. The most natural path to certainty is to get a job. That is also how we initially ceded control to our need for certainty some 12,000 years ago. We became an agrarian society and inserted ourselves into what would eventually become the monotony of the modern workday.

You might say that is just how the world works, but it *didn't* work that way when your Boss Brain evolved, nor did it work that way for 99.94% of our existence. Technology advanced and societies became more complicated, but human instinct and the desire for independence have not changed. All of this began on the very first farm, and it continues today.

THE WALLS OF ADEQUACY

Of all the farms that sprang up twelve centuries ago, one grew faster than any other and became the first settlement of more than 2000 people.

That village would eventually become the longest permanently inhabited settlement in the world. Ideally positioned on fertile plains between protective mountains and a wide river, it was a paradise of sun and soil. The land around the village held the magical combination of natural defenses, fertile soil, abundant sunshine, and fresh water.

Generation after generation expanded the site's natural ability to support massive amounts of food. Its inhabitants recognized their wealth of resources and feared losing them. So, they erected enormous walls around their city. Eventually, all the inhabitants began to fear the unknown perils that lay outside the walls of what they called Jericho.

More than ten thousand years after its birth, the walled city of Jericho was as it had always been. It was a beautiful and crowded oasis filled with fearful occupants, some of whom had never been outside the city walls. The population grew from two thousand to ten thousand. Each year, everyone was forced to subsist on less and less. Everyone in the city was bound by the walls of Jericho.

However, Jericho's walls were nothing more than an inconvenience for invaders. Indeed, the city was conquered six times before the Roman Empire arrived in 70 AD. Despite being the oldest continuously inhabited city in the world, Jericho was not even their intended prize. The Roman army was only there to use Jericho's resources as part of their supply line to invade and conquer Jerusalem.

The fear of losing what little they had forced Jericho to play a role in someone else's conquest. They helped make someone else's optimistic vision of the future a reality, not their own. Like frontline employees of a huge multinational corporation, whatever mediocre existence they scraped out was determined by those they served. They no longer controlled their own destiny. They became cogs in the wheels of an empire.

THE CAGE OF COMFORT

Modern entrepreneurs face the same decision that the citizens of Jericho faced. They could live on the relative certainty of limited provisions, or they could explore the limits of their potential outside the walls of society. Each year, the costs of survival grew. Yet their productivity was bound by the barriers they built around themselves.

Here is the most telling example of how the desire for certainty limits long-term potential: Jericho was founded 5,000 years before Rome. Jericho had a comfortable head start, yet it could not withstand pressures from the ever-advancing outside world. The citizens of Jericho found comfort in predictable adequacy, which made them complacent and halted their advancement.

Yale researchers have revealed how predictability creates complacency and limits the brain's natural ability to learn and grow. In their initial experiment, monkeys chose between pressing a red button that provided rewards 80% of the time and a green button that paid off 20% of the time. The monkeys quickly learned that the red button paid rewards more frequently and stopped hitting the green button.

Then the scientists switched things up a bit. In the second experiment, the red button paid out 80 percent of the time. But the green buttons were unpredictable—the frequency and size of the yielded rewards always varied. When the monkeys decided that the green button held no predictability, they abandoned it for the red.[8]

The researchers measured the monkeys' brain activity while they played with all the buttons. A clear pattern emerged. If the monkeys could predict how often a button paid rewards, brain regions associated with learning shut down. When the monkeys couldn't anticipate the frequency or size of the treat, their learning centers lit up. However, when the monkeys figured out which buttons were predictable, they stopped pressing the other buttons.

Once the brain discerns the easiest way to generate consistent rewards in a given environment, two things happen. First, learning and developing new techniques becomes pointless. And second, you become less likely to test another environment. You stop pressing other buttons and build walls to protect your frequent and consistent reward. Predictability spawns complacency. If you're not at least a little stressed about the outcome of your efforts, your brain stops learning.

As one of the Yale neuroscientists put it, "Perhaps the most important insight from our study is that the function of the brain as well as the

---

8. Bart Massi, et al, "Volatility Facilitates Value Updating in the Prefrontal Cortex" *Neuron*, 99(3), 598–608.e4. https://doi.org/10.1016/j.neuron.2018.06.033.

nature of learning is not fixed, but adapts according to the stability of the environment . . . When you enter a more novel and volatile environment, this might enhance the tendency for the brain to absorb more information." Uncertainty signals that you're unsure of your environment or skills, and your brain's learning centers kick into overdrive.

Entrepreneurs still live and work within the confines of the metaphorical walls of society. There is no escaping that fact. But entrepreneurs cannot stop learning; they cannot stop pressing other buttons. Consistent rewards may tempt you to build physical and mental walls around your growth. However, once you abandon learning and experimentation, you give control over to whoever or whatever offers the most predictability.

Once you abandon learning and experimentation, you give control over to whoever or whatever offers the most predictability.

A predictable paycheck represents the limited provisions produced within the walls of employment. It is Jericho's red button.

MONEY, LEGACY, AND OPTIMISM

In 2018, Bill Gates became the first-ever guest editor of *Time* magazine. As a philanthropist, humanitarian, and one of the richest people in the world, he could have chosen any number of subjects as the theme for his issue. He chose to focus the entire issue on what he sees as the most important topic for society today: optimism.

Gates admits that it is easy to feel like the world is falling apart. However, the billionaire argues that despite all the terrible tragedies that make the news, the world is better than ever before and is still getting better. Gates says, "I'm not trying to downplay the work that remains. Being an optimist doesn't mean you ignore tragedy and injustice," he explains. "It means you're inspired to look for people making progress on those fronts and to help spread that progress." According to Gates, there is a disconnect between reality and society's pessimistic sentiments.

Gates isn't alone in his view of the future. A recent study interviewed millionaire and billionaire self-made entrepreneurs to assess their dominant personality traits. More than eight out of ten assessed themselves as optimistic, and 78% ranked themselves very optimistic. Nearly 85% strongly rejected the statement, "I see myself as more of a pessimist."[9] Among them, no other personality trait was as prevalent as optimism.

The way the interviewees use the word *optimist* correlated to self-efficacy or the belief in their abilities to achieve a goal or overcome challenging situations. In their own words, optimism is a kind of resourcefulness, "a result of your own abilities, the network you have cultivated or your intellect, you are always able to identify solutions and to overcome anything." It doesn't mean that they naively believe in the inevitability of a happy ending. They understand that unforeseen challenges will always arise. Still, they have confidence in themselves and their ability to prevail over the hurdles that lie between them and their goal.

The same theme reveals itself across time—belief in themselves and a willingness to explore their abilities. The interviewees were all self-made men and women. They didn't inherit their wealth, and they were not naively optimistic. But they did turn their inherent optimism into action. They envisioned a better future for themselves and their families and made that vision a reality.

There is little difference between those who crossed continents searching for a better life and those who dare to define the role they play in the modern world. Their optimistic Boss Brains inspired action. The accumulation of wealth was merely a by-product of building a satisfactory legacy, not the legacy itself.

THE SOURCE OF THE ENTREPRENEURSHIP GAP

The ability to envision a future of bountiful harvests and times of plenty is a powerful motivator. Why risk being eaten by a saber-toothed tiger when you can sit by a fire in your hut with a full belly? And why risk starting a company and being your own boss when you can accept a predictable role and collect a paycheck? The idea itself is simple and linear: stay

---

9. Rainer Zitelmann. *The Wealth Elite: A Groundbreaking Study of the Psychology of the Super Rich*. London: LID, 2019.

in one safe, comfortable place and create abundance instead of searching for it. Then and now, that idea produces unintended consequences.

As Yuval Harari noted in his book *Sapiens*, the Agricultural Revolution did not herald in an era of "easy living." Instead, it caused a population explosion and created class divisions. Farmers worked harder than foragers and had worse diets. Permanent settlements became hotbeds for infectious diseases. Huge amounts of stored food tempted thieves, so walls were built and guarded. According to Harari, "the Agricultural Revolution was history's biggest fraud."

The unintended consequences of farming prevented the better future it attempted to create. With a poor diet, wretched living conditions, disease, and class divisions, it was predictably bad. But predictable, nonetheless.

The bias to hate uncertainty even more than predictably negative consequences is ingrained into the modern brain. The tendency to choose the predictable option, however fraught with misery it may be, battles our optimistic instinct to search for a better future.

It is the modern human enigma: comply with the collective and face a predictable monotonous future that is sometimes ripe with pain and suffering. Or defy societal expectations and face an uncertain future potentially filled with happiness and meaning. The hardwired instincts of the Boss Brain battle the opposing software of the modern brain. The subsequent conflicting emotions yield the turmoil that we all feel as a witness to and participant in today's society.

Without frontiers to explore and uncharted territories to discover, we have fashioned a cell for ourselves. It might not have visible bars, but it does create mental and physical barriers. This self-made prison is like a merry-go-round that moves only in one direction and always begins and ends in the same place. As nearly all quality of life metrics rise around the globe, jumping off that comfortable merry-go-round is getting harder with each generation.

The inner war between optimism and uncertainty is the source of the entrepreneurship gap. Battle lines are drawn between what we want and what we have, between predictability and possibility. Each year, more and more American workers become metaphorical casualties in this war, choosing certainty over optimism. They choose consistent adequacy. Then their brain shuts off, and they spend the rest of their lives pressing one button.

WHY DOES THIS MATTER?

The modern world is just an extension of that very first farm. Most employees actually enjoy what their ancestors envisioned—a relatively safe work environment, consistent schedules, and predictable rewards. Modern employment also yields a cache of unintended consequences, but that is not why aspiring entrepreneurs quit their jobs. An optimistic vision of the future and a belief in their ability to make that vision a reality inspires their actions.

This is why early humans quickly scattered themselves around the globe over difficult terrain and in extreme weather conditions. Nothing was certain. So, they constantly searched for ways to improve their existence. And not just in incremental ways, like warmer clothes or more comfortable beds; they fearlessly embraced massive change and enormous cultural shifts. Always challenging themselves. Never settling for the status quo.

The inner war between optimism and uncertainty is the source of the entrepreneurship gap.

Without optimism, our rise would have been concentric and methodical, slowly spiraling outward in safe and predictable ways. But that isn't what happened. Instead, small bands of our ancestors shot out into the world on aggressive trajectories. Nothing but optimism could have propelled them over mountain ranges and frozen tundra.

Optimism was the spark that lit fire to our entrepreneurial instincts. It was the catalyst that Mother Nature needed to mold us. Optimism empowers us to choose which walls to work within and where to set boundaries. The Boss Brain doesn't recognize the conflict between optimism and uncertainty because it evolved when there was no certainty. There wasn't a predictable, consistent option. Belief in a better future and in one's own ability to make that vision a reality was the only sure thing.

The illusion of certainty has deceived the modern brain. It has been bribed to operate within the boundaries that someone else pays you to stay within, to hit one button all day long, every day. Just like the citizens of Jericho, your efforts serve the supply line in someone else's conquest. In exchange for that sacrifice, you receive nothing more than predictable adequacy.

KEY POINTS

- The conflict between your instinctive optimism and your disdain for uncertainty is the source of the entrepreneurship gap.
- Even paradise can become a prison.
- Societal expectations are walls that limit your ability to maximize your potential.
- To achieve predictability, you are forced to sacrifice opportunity.

QUESTIONS TO ASK

- Does this action bring me one step closer to my goals, or am I doing this because it makes life more predictable?
- Have I built walls around my current conditions which limit me to only incremental advancements?
- How can I create my vision of the distant future, even if life in the near term is less certain?
- Has my need for certainty limited my willingness or ability to learn and develop?

CHAPTER 2

BE YOURSELF

"EVERY MAN IS THE ARCHITECT OF HIS OWN FORTUNE."
—SALLUST

Christopher Knight was only 20 years old when he walked into the wilderness of Maine. There he lived alone without human contact for almost three decades.

Before that, he grew up in a very close family with four older brothers and a younger sister. Christopher, like all the Knight children, was brilliant. They were all technically skilled and curious by nature. They spent their days learning and testing new ideas and their nights reading Shakespeare and other poetry.

The Knight family wasn't wealthy, but they were studious and industrious. Chris and his siblings studied thermodynamics and decided to build a greenhouse. They buried hundreds of gallons of water in one-gallon containers beneath it. They knew that water molecules gather heat during the day and at night released that heat. So, throughout the Maine winter, the Knight family grew food in their greenhouse without paying a dime to the electric company or grocers.

Despite—or perhaps because of—his intelligence, Christopher felt he never really fit into modern society. He decided to walk away from civilization because there was no role for him to fill that didn't feel like a farce, like he was living someone else's life. He was not content with the options society offered. Like each of us, Chris yearned for true freedom and liberty. So, at the age of 20, he drove his car into a remote area of the wilderness in Maine, left his car keys on the center console, and walked into the woods. He lived there without human contact for 27 years.

When asked, Knight couldn't accurately describe what it felt like to live alone, having no contact with society for more than a quarter of a century. "It's complicated. Solitude increased my perception. But here's the tricky thing: when I applied my increased perception to myself, I lost my identity. There was no audience, no one to perform for. There was no need to define me. I became irrelevant."

The dividing line between Knight's identity and the forest dissolved. He said, "My desires dropped away. I didn't long for anything. I didn't even have a name. To put it romantically, I was completely free."

Knight's story evokes varied emotions. Some think it's crazy. Others understand and often romanticize his story for their own reasons. In today's world, outliers are often shunned, mocked, and excluded. When a person chooses to walk a different path, they open themselves to judgment and ridicule.

However, reactions to Chris's story not only teach us something about society, but they also tell us something about ourselves. We all know what it is like to be late for work and stuck in traffic after a long week, to work all year just to squeeze out two weeks of quality time with loved ones, and to spend more time *maintaining* life than living it. We know what it's like to follow society's rules but still feel like we're missing something. To do everything that we are *supposed* to do yet remain unfulfilled and unhappy. But Chris Knight wasn't searching for happiness; he was escaping unhappiness. He sought the freedom to become the most authentic version of himself, not who society expected him to be. Once he had eliminated all the environmental clues that previously defined him, he found that freedom.

The question we should be asking ourselves isn't, "Why did Chris choose to defy social expectations and carve his own path?" The question we should be asking is, "Why don't more of us make the same choice?"

WHO DO YOU THINK YOU ARE?

Imagine that you are hiking a mountain trail in Maine with your best friend on a beautiful day and see Chris Knight walking in the woods. He's disheveled and unshaven. His clothes are tattered and stained. He doesn't look like someone who is merely hiking in the woods. He looks like the woods are his home, like some wild man lost to time. Most likely, you would turn to your friend and ask, "Who is that guy?" Even though Mr. Knight had let go of who he was, you would still expect him to have a name and an identity. So, you would ask, "*who* was that?" not "*what* was that?"

Now, imagine that you are hiking the same mountain trail with your best friend when up ahead, you see a green alien that is seven feet tall with six legs. It walks toward you and says, "I'm sorry if I startled you. I was just out for a morning stroll. My name is Bob. Nice to meet you. Have a nice day." Bob then spreads thin leathery wings and flies away.

Would you turn to your friend and ask *who* that was? Probably not. Even though the creature had a name, was self-aware, polite, and well-spoken, you would most likely ask your friend, "*What* was that?" The ability to speak, interact and feel empathy is not enough, at least in our minds, for the creature to have an identity. Bob was out of place—in the wrong environment. Our environment doesn't just determine what we see, it also determines how we see it. A person wearing a trench coat in the city on a cold winter day would blend in. The same person wearing the same coat on the beach would immediately draw attention.

We subconsciously use clues from the environment to determine an identity for ourselves and others. Therefore, after we ran into Bob on the trail, we would ask *what* instead of *who*. If Bob took you to his alien planet, all of the members of his species would look at you and ask, "What is that?" Because you would be out of *your* environment.

The subtle difference reveals the depth of how your surroundings and circumstances create who you think you are. Your name, nationality, and even your language result from where and when you were born; they are not fundamental elements of *what you are*. If you were born in Virginia in 1740, you would likely consider yourself to be British. Fifty years later, you would probably call yourself American. So, who are you? The question is both existential and philosophical.

Today, we construct our entire identities from the role we play in the world around us. We allow society to determine who we are and what we do with our lives. That is why a child in Montana is statistically more likely to want to be a cowboy than a child in New York. Cowboys are everywhere in Montana, and kids want to emulate their environment.

> *Today, we construct our entire identities from the role we play in the world around us. We allow society to determine who we are and what we do with our lives.*

A recent study of American parents with children who are eleven or younger showed that 81% use YouTube to find content for their kids to watch.[1] And 34% of those parents say their children watch content on YouTube regularly. The effect is significant. The same percentage, or a third of those kids, indicated that they wanted to be a YouTuber when they grew up. They are inundated with YouTubers and want to emulate their environment.

Whether they want to be cowboys or You-Tubers, both sets of kids are products of their environments and not just in who they think they are, but also in who they aspire to become.

The anomaly of transcending your circumstances and becoming something other than what society expects is exceedingly rare. So rare that Hollywood makes movies about those who rise to greatness despite being born into poverty-stricken, uneducated families. Awards are given to those who defy their circumstances and their environments. We herald them as heroes, and that celebration is a nod to our hidden desires, a confirmation of our envy. We all hope to differentiate ourselves by exceeding society's expectations.

On a biological level, we are nearly identical to ancient humans. The most primitive parts of our brains are devoid of an environmentally

---

1. Aaron Smith and Monica Anderson, "Social Media Use in 2018," Pew Research Center viewed at https://www.pewresearch.org/internet/2018/03/01/social-media-use-in-2018/.

designed identity. That is what we are, not who we are. Ultimately, we are just a character built from clues in the world we were born into, even though we played no part in designing that world. Our identities are mutually agreed-upon fiction, and most of us live our whole lives within its imaginary boundaries.

WHAT DO YOU THINK YOU ARE?

One of the more famous lines from Jack Nicholson's character in the movie *The Departed* is, "I don't want to be a product of my environment. I want my environment to be a product of me." If you are an employee, your employer controls nearly every aspect of your life and many aspects of your environment. Most people reject this statement initially, but they eventually accept it to be true. Don't believe it? Think about it. What time you wake, when you eat, how much you earn, where you live, where you shop, who you spend your days with, and how each day is structured are all controlled by the type and location of your job.

Pretend for a moment that you are Katelyn Miller, a 32-year-old West Virginian of Irish descent, a lawyer, a Methodist, and an outspoken defender of the workplace rights of coal miners. Your modern brain has constructed an identity made up entirely of external variables. Would you defend the rights of coal miners if you had been born in Alaska? Are you somehow genetically different because you are of Irish descent? Does your DNA make you Methodist? Of course not. Each descriptor is a by-product of the role Katelyn plays within the time and place of her birth. Katelyn's identity was constructed for her before she was even born. However, she was able to make one choice. She was able to choose the role she would play, but only from the options that were made readily available to her. And that choice became as much a part of who she is as her birthplace.

The entire façade of identity is so widely accepted that even our language depicts our submission to it. In English, we say: *I am a financial advisor, I am a truck driver,* and *I am a teacher.* We do not say: *I advise, I drive,* or *I teach.* Even the Spanish language describes careers with the verb *ser,* not the verb *estar.* "Soy un Profesor." *Ser* describes an unchangeable quality. *Estar* describes something that can change. The language of

> *Your identity will either be an asset or a liability on the journey to entrepreneurship.*

the modern brain defines what you are based on what you do. Telling someone to "be yourself" is just saying that they should feel free to choose from among the options that their environment has made readily available.

Your identity will either be an asset or a liability on the journey to entrepreneurship. If you perceive yourself to be a product of your environment, then your identity becomes a liability. However, if your environment is a product of your identity, it will always be an asset.

IDENTITY, TANGIBILITY, AND SOCIAL RELATIVITY

All the tactical steps that create and start a business are just tasks. They are not a business strategy in and of themselves. Most of it is busy work: establishing operational entities, filing for employer identification numbers, obtaining licensing, setting up an accounting system, etc. None of these steps creates an actual tangible result. That's because the system is designed to process information, not to produce a profit. Profits must be manufactured, created where once there was nothing. Money is the by-product of that creation and your productivity. In business and life, there are times when you process and times when you produce, but you are only paid for what you produce.

Most entrepreneurship lessons focus purely on processing information while ignoring real productivity. For instance, what does your business do? What does it sell? What service does it provide? What problem does it solve? And then there's the *how* questions. How do you sell your product? Is it online or in a brick-and-mortar location? How do you find customers? How do you market your services? These are all common, if not clichéd, questions in the business world.

The first step toward entrepreneurship is not to define what you do and how you do it. The market will dictate that. The first step toward entrepreneurship is to define who and why. Who is your customer, and why do they need you? Both are critical questions to answer. But more importantly, who are you, and why are you doing this? When answering these questions, it is crucial to remember that money is a tool. It is the by-product of your productivity. It is not a reason. Money cannot be your why.

Half the world's population lives on less than \$5.50/day, while the average American lives on between \$92 and \$200/day, depending on age. If your net worth is more than \$93,000, you are already in the top 10% of the wealthiest people on the planet. The individual poverty level in the U.S. for 2019 is around \$12,000, while the median global income is less than \$10,000. In other words, the poorest people in America still earn more than half of the world's population.

The vast majority of aspiring entrepreneurs in America have never left the country. Therefore, their perspective on wealth is socially relative. Social relativity skews opinions and creates biases. There will always be someone with a bigger house and a nicer car. On the global stage, wealth is so completely relative that it is impossible to use income as a benchmark for maximizing potential. That is why it is imperative to discard your environmentally implied perception of self and find your own why—one that transcends social relativity.

ELEPHANTS AND NIKE

Ecologists recently discovered an interesting by-product of the destruction wrought by hungry elephants. Biodiversity is richer and more complex within elephant feeding grounds than in the untouched jungle. While accessing the tastiest and most nutritious greens, elephants often dig up the ground, tear off branches, and even knock over large trees.

It is not difficult to recognize where elephants have fed; the area is trampled and chaotic. To the human eye, the beauty is gone. It no longer looks like pristine, untouched nature. However, in the eyes of smaller animals and reptiles, elephant feeding grounds look like an eclectic community with limitless amenities. Fallen trees make perfect dens for little ones and even better places to hide from predators. All the ground clutter invites insects and rodents on which small animals can feed. Tender blades of grass that carpet the newly exposed jungle floor are nurtured by unimpeded sunlight beaming in where tree canopies once darkened the ground. Elephants, it seems, are environmental engineers.

Like elephants, entrepreneurs manufacture their environments for themselves and others. Traffic patterns follow access to trade areas, and symbiotic brands support each other through shared co-tenancy. Entire social structures, like schools, churches, and neighborhoods, emerge from shared access to entrepreneurial resources. And just like elephants, when entrepreneurs have maximized the opportunities that a particular area offers, they move on to new opportunities, breaking ground for future development.

Elephants also have complex social structures, just like humans. They recognize each other after being separated for extended periods and often examine the bones of deceased friends and loved ones. Elephants understand who they are, but their importance to the surrounding economy of resources is defined by what they are. For budding entrepreneurs, understanding the difference between who and what ensures that we move on to new opportunities when it's time.

Phil Knight, iconic former CEO and co-founder of Nike, explained the power of "what" over "who" in his book *Shoe Dog*:

> Sometimes you have to give up. Sometimes knowing when to give up, when to try something else, is genius. Giving up doesn't mean stopping. Don't ever stop.

If an entrepreneur considers herself a restauranteur, she may overlook opportunities outside the restaurant industry even if her business is failing. She isn't a restauranteur; she is an entrepreneur who, at this time, happens to own a restaurant. By thinking of herself as a restauranteur, she is unknowingly accepting a place within the roles that society has offered. She has not knocked over trees or disrupted the ecology.

Before founding Nike, Phil Knight was a sports reporter, an accountant, and even a university professor. If he had allowed his identity to be defined by what he did during that time, Nike might never have existed. Both Chris Knight and Phil Knight, along with all entrepreneurs, manufacture their environments and create opportunities for themselves and others where previously none existed. They accomplish this by ignoring who they are and knowing when to move on and find more opportunities to be what they are.

WHY DOES THIS MATTER?

Making the mental transition into entrepreneurship requires more than behavioral modification; it requires identity transformation. Your Boss Brain doesn't recognize the social constructs of your environment as part of your identity. Your entrepreneurial instincts originate from the most primal parts of your brain, not from modern economic pressures. That's why the desire to be your own boss is as prevalent among the highest-paid employees as it is among everyone else. A bigger salary will not change what you are.

To ignore your drive to create a legacy is to deny the most fundamental element of your humanity.

If you are a dissatisfied American worker who wants to quit and be your own boss, your dissatisfaction isn't only with your actual station in life. You are also unhappy because the role you play within the options that America provides doesn't allow you to maximize your inherent abilities. Your identity is, therefore, the foundation of your motivation. The geography and timing of your existence offered different choices than those offered to your ancestors. Still, they don't change your innate human desire to explore the limits of your potential.

The world says that you should be yourself while your Boss Brain rejects the hierarchy of the modern workplace and the limited choices it provides. Rather than ignoring them, the budding entrepreneur must nurture their instincts through fearless trial and the inevitable error. To ignore your drive to create a legacy is to deny the most fundamental element of your humanity.

To your Boss Brain, what you do is a by-product of what you are, not vice versa. In the animal kingdom, lions hunt, birds fly, and fish swim. What they are defines what they do. Sometimes birds hunt, but that does not make them lions. Sometimes lions swim, but that does not make them fish. The Boss Brain ignores the environmental clues that dictate identity. It gives no thought to who. Who you are is for others to perceive and define for themselves, but that does not change what you are.

This is a primary distinction between the employee mindset and the Boss Brain: one looks at its environment and takes a place within it, while the other creates the world in which it lives.

KEY POINTS

- It is not enough to envision a better future for yourself. You also have to trust your ability to make it so. You have to trust in your self-efficacy.
- True freedom to explore the limits of your potential only comes when you separate who you are from what you do and vice versa.
- You are an entrepreneur, first and foremost. When, why, and how you act on those instincts is secondary.
- Don't allow who you think you are to limit your willingness to seize an opportunity.
- Neither your self-perception nor your environment has the power to change what you are at a primal level.

QUESTIONS TO ASK

- Do I really trust in myself?
- Do I want to be my own boss, or would I rather construct a life that is consistent with what society expects from me?
- Do I make life decisions based on my own desires or based on my relative status within society?
- Am I humble enough to give up on a failing project, learn from those lessons, and continue elsewhere?
- Am I a product of my environment? Or is my environment a product of me?

CHAPTER 3

FOLLOW YOUR DREAMS

"I AM THE MASTER OF MY FATE, I AM THE
CAPTAIN OF MY SOUL."
—WILLIAM E HENLEY, INVICTUS

In 20 BC, Emperor Caesar Augustus, the first emperor of the Roman Empire, erected a marble and gilded bronze monument in the Roman Forum. It was called the *Milliarium Aureum*, or the Golden Milestone. At its peak, the Roman Empire stretched from Great Britain to Egypt and from Spain to Syria. All the roads that snaked through the 1.7 million square mile empire were said to begin at this monument, and the distance to each empirical city was measured from it. As a result, the common phrase "all roads lead to Rome" was born.

But what if Rome wasn't your dream destination? What if, unlike everyone else, you sought a future outside the empire's control? What if your destiny was not to fill an empirical role that perpetuated Roman rule? Instead, what if you wanted to live life on different terms, measuring success only by achievement relative to *your* abilities? Once beyond the edges of the empire, you would have to build your own roads.

We tell each other from our earliest days that we can choose our destination in life—that we can do whatever we want to do, live however we want to live. As children, that sentiment fuels our passions. As a child without worry, fear, money, or debt, it is easy to see only possibilities and conjure fanciful, even miraculous, ideas of what the future holds.

However, not long after conjuring big dreams, we are given a conflicting message. Students are told to temper their passion and focus on good grades so they can attend a respected university. And just when they gain a glimpse of freedom and empowerment, their college advisors counsel pragmatism. Students are lectured continuously on choosing a stable and predictable career. They must first earn a degree and find a good job that will hopefully fund their passions.

Modern culture claims to support empowerment and individualism. However, the entire education system is designed to assimilate you into the workforce. For example, there are more than 5,300 colleges and universities in America. Virtually all of them offer training for job interviews and assistance with resume preparation. Entire departments are dedicated to job placement, with dozens of people working furiously to place you within a pre-existing role in the workforce. However, only 4%—or about 230—of these institutions offer entrepreneurship or small business as a major, and most of these programs began in the last 20 years.

Across all majors, 77% of college students and 72% of high school students recently indicated that they want to start their own businesses immediately after college. However, you might be surprised to learn that a higher percentage of those who did not attend college are self-employed. In fact, an American without a high school diploma is 20% more likely to be self-employed than someone with a master's degree.[1]

In the absence of employment opportunities made available by formal education, a higher percentage of people are pushed into entrepreneurship. By going to college, you are statistically more likely to choose from among the options society has presented to you than you are to carve out a role for yourself. The entrepreneurship void in higher education sends a clear message: society expects each citizen to fill a predefined position, to take their place in the spinning cogs of the empire.

---

1. Steven F. Hipple and Laurel A. Hammond, "Self-employment in the United States," Bureau of Labor Statistics viewed at https://www.bls.gov/spotlight/2016/self-employment-in-the-united-states/home.htm.

CONFLICTING MESSAGES

Even outside the prestigious halls of our colleges and universities, our society is saturated with the expectation of assimilation disguised as otherwise nurturing messages: it's okay to have dreams, but only if they are realistic and widely accepted as normal. Be who you want to be, but only if that person is consistent with your neighbors and peers. Aspire to greatness, but don't take unnecessary risks. Follow your heart, but you must also follow the predetermined path defined by society, i.e., go to school, get a job, and buy a house.

Sound familiar? We are bombarded with conflicting messages like these from the time we can talk. They are the wolves of integration masquerading as the sheep of encouragement. An entrepreneur must not only overcome the hurdles of starting and building a business, but each must also endure the ridicule and the doubt that their refusal to assimilate incites. It is society's cruelest and most heartless version of bait-and-switch—to preach the positivity of individualism and then judge you negatively for non-conformity.

It is society's cruelest and most heartless version of bait-and-switch—to preach the positivity of individualism and then judge you negatively for non-conformity.

Society's conflicting messages are made even more sinister by the peculiar rise and fall of optimism throughout your life. Most people might suspect that optimism is a childish quality and that as you grow older, you grow more pessimistic. Media and movies are ripe with stereotypical portrayals of crabby old folks pitted against unrealistically positive and rebellious youth. But that is not what science has revealed.

Researchers plotted the trajectory of optimism across the human lifespan. They found optimism to be the lowest among those in their twenties. It then rises steadily through their thirties and forties, peaking in the mid-fifties.

Specifically, people experience their highest levels of optimism at age fifty-five.[2]

Optimism levels follow an inverted U-shape with a peak in late midlife. It appears that people need time for good things to happen. Positive life events raise our optimism, but negative events do not necessarily detract from it. In your twenties, you haven't had time to build a library of good experiences to reference. But that is the age when we make some of our most crucial life decisions. Therefore, we are least optimistic at the precise moment in our lives when we most need optimism.

Entrepreneurship is most accessible before we have saddled ourselves with debt and obligation and before we have children. With our lowest levels of optimism, would-be entrepreneurs in their twenties choose the safer, more predictable route—the road that society laid out for them.

At the height of the Roman Empire, all roads led to one destination. Today, one road supposedly leads to all destinations. The mere implication is preposterous. That way of thinking took root during the postwar economic boom of the 1940s, when America needed workers. It is an antiquated mentality that creates one thing and one thing only . . . employees.

THE REAL AMERICAN DREAM

In 1931, the historian James Truslow Adams first defined the American Dream in his book *Epic of America*. In it, he declared that "the American Dream is that dream of a land in which life should be better and richer and fuller for everyone, with opportunity for each according to ability." Adams was quick to point out that the American Dream was not "motor cars and high wages." To him, it was a social order where each person could achieve everything that is within their innate ability.

Alone, the American Dream might sound more like a sales pitch. But coupled with the U.S. Constitution, which protected each person's right to the pursuit of happiness, the stage was set for a society that appealed to everyone who aspired to live a better life. The Constitution formally protects every American's right to improve their life. Our forefathers knew that this was the best way to ensure liberty, freedom, and, most importantly, economic growth.

---

2. Ted Schwaba, et al, "Optimism Development Across Adulthood and Associations with Positive and Negative Life Events," *Social Psychological and Personality Science*, 10(8), 1092–1101.

The story is well known. Entrepreneurial immigrants poured into Ellis Island, causing self-employment rates to top 20%. Being your own boss was the original American Dream. Then came the post-WWII economic boom, suburban sprawl, and affordable housing. For the first time, homeownership was within reach of the exploding middle class. And what's the easiest way to get approved for a home mortgage? Work a steady job.

The housing crisis of 2008 is brutal evidence of how important the homeowner narrative is to the American economy. The American Dream was distorted into exactly what Adams said it wasn't: cars, high wages, and homes. We work our entire lives to obtain these things because we have forgotten the *real* definition of the American Dream—to maximize our freedom and achieve everything that is within our innate ability.

SELLING THE NEW DREAM

Selling the new American Dream meant selling materialism as a substitute for happiness. Nothing dulls the pain of monotony and the loss of control like new toys. Coincidentally, all this happened right when televisions became readily available. Advertisements cranked messages about all the things a modern family needed to be happy. It was a constant flow of must-haves and gadgetry meant to eliminate every struggle and make life easy. Consumerism was born, and television was the perfect medium to show you exactly how to live happily and fulfilled.

Choose Happiness, Open Happiness, Drink Happiness, Visit Happiness, Own your own Piece of Happiness, Drive Happiness—the clichéd list of ads selling happiness goes on and on without end to this very day. Only now, the average American family is not watching ads on one black and white TV in their living room. Today, U.S. households own an average of eleven connected devices, including seven with screens, to view content. Self-employment has decreased virtually every year since TV became commonplace in American homes and businesses. Americans stopped creating companies and started consuming products. Consumption replaced creation.

If employment dictates nearly every aspect of your life and your environment, media content controls what remains. Ads tell you what food to buy, what clothes to wear, and what car to drive. Your preferences follow you around the Internet, flashing ads for the things you desire most. By the time you finish school, get a job, and buy a house, a cycle is created. Consumption increases debt; debt increases the need for a predictably adequate income; the daily monotony of predictable adequacy increases unhappiness; and unhappiness increases the need for consumption. The story of your life is written in this cycle.

The American Dream was once a mountain of opportunity that anyone could climb. You could fall and always get back up and continue climbing. Now, the dream is like a hole with a buy-with-one-click button at the bottom. You climb in, not up. And the more items shipped to you, the harder it is to climb out.

VOLUNTARY SERVITUDE

A few decades before the word *entrepreneur* first appeared, a scholar and philosopher named Michel de Montaigne penned essays that would eventually launch modern liberalism. This was not liberalism as a po-litical platform as it is today—quite the opposite. Montaigne's writings focused on individual freedom completely detached from any political or social action. His writings advocated for the rule of private individual judgment over governmental systems or schools of thought. He recog-nized that the things we believe are, by and large, part of the customs of the society in which we live.

He and a friend often wrote about our voluntary servitude to the social hierarchy, the church, and the state. Montaigne asserted that we choose our paths out of adherence to social nuances, not out of the pur-suit of personal convictions. "The laws of conscience, which we say are born from nature, are born of custom. Each man, holding in inward veneration the opinions and the behavior approved and accepted around him, cannot break loose from them without remorse, or apply himself to them without self-satisfaction."[3] Custom not only guides your behavior but also reassures you that social conformity is the right choice.

The most ruthless aspect of custom is its invisibility. Montaigne wrote that we "wrongly take that which appears for that which is."[4] What

3. Marc Foglia, Marc and Emiliano Ferrari, "Michel de Montaigne", The Stanford Encyclopedia of Philosophy (Winter 2019 Edition), Edward N. Zalta (ed.), URL = <https://plato.stanford.edu/archives/win2019/entries/montaigne/>.

4. Ibid.

we are immersed in becomes invisible—like a scuba diver tossed by the current but cannot see the water. This is why a crime in one society can be considered perfectly normal behavior in another. Citizens of every culture think that the laws they use to frame their thoughts and actions are born from nature, but they are built on customs. We are born with our own will, but we are not born with an innate understanding of society's expectations. Therefore, customs are the opposite of being free. We learn them. They are part of the modern software that gets loaded onto our ancient human hardware.

Customs and cultural expectations saturate society. Parenting, education, politics, entertainment, religion, and occupation are all tossed by the invisible tide of what is customary. The modern brain succumbs to the illusions of colloquial reality and cultural morality.

> *The most ruthless aspect of custom is its invisibility.*

In American culture, customs have the added complexity of being completely contradictory. The U.S. touts entrepreneurship as the thread that wove the fabric of American culture. Simultaneously, we tell each other that the American Dream lies at the end of a single predetermined path. What is widely expected of citizens in modern-day America would be considered voluntary servitude by the Hindu Monks who were the original inspiration for the word *entrepreneur* in the 17th century.

THE STORY OF YOUR LIFE

Entrepreneurship means writing your own life story. But a person's life story is not necessarily biographic. There are facts and events; however, how a person integrates them is what creates their story. What tends to happen is a person picks events and weaves them together to create meaning in the present. This narrative helps establish identity.

The things you choose worthy of including in your story shape your self-image. But a life story doesn't just describe events; it reveals why those events are important. The story tells you who you are and why, which also affects who you'll become. As one researcher put it, "Life is incredibly complex . . . to hold onto our experience, we need to make meaning out of it. The way we do that is by structuring our lives into stories."[5]

As you age, consistent themes develop. In the story's last chapters, those themes become more rigid. Researchers think the gradual process of developing themes is the result of layering three aspects of yourself. At birth, you are an "actor" in the role into which you were born. In adolescence, you become an "agent," making your own decisions. The final layer is "author." This is when themes solidify and mold the past, present, and future into a narrative—the story of your life.

The problem with this layering is people weave cultural cues into their stories. Cultural expectations become embedded into a person's master narrative. For better or worse, they serve as assembly instructions for people who use them to build their own stories. The upside for children is assembly instructions help them understand the trajectory of life. But there are two massive downsides to these cultural narratives. First, they stigmatize anyone who doesn't use them to build their story. Second, they create unrealistic expectations of happiness for those who do.

College, traditional employment, homeownership, and consumerism are all cultural narratives. The assembly instructions for an American life can be summarized into "go to school, get a job, buy a house, and a nice car." You may write the details in your life story, but society structured the plot. It is the blueprint for mediocrity.

WHEN WILL I NEED TO KNOW THIS?

Thankfully, the entrepreneurial spirit of America is still alive and well among high school students. A full 72% want to start their own business after college. However, a whopping 84% say that high school did not prepare them for handling personal finances. A recent survey revealed that high school graduates listed the STEM subjects as the courses that provided the least value to them in their personal and professional lives. STEM subjects make up only 13% of today's jobs.

More than 75% of students also indicated personal finance classes should be mandatory in high school. Sixty-eight percent want stock

5. D. P. McAdams & E. Manczak, "Personality and the life story" In M. Mikulincer, & P. R. Shaver (Eds.), APA Handbook of Personality and Social Psychology: Volume 4: Personality Processes and Individual Differences Washington, DC: American Psychological Association Press, 2015, 425-446.

market basics added to their curriculum. Nearly 60% also support adding courses on how to file taxes.[6]

As they move into post-secondary education, students will find that college has significant value. However, it does not provide the *instant* value that most assume. It is perfect if you have a particular goal, and college is the only way to achieve that goal, like law or medical school. Generally speaking, college graduates consistently occupy higher-paying jobs than non-college graduates, and more education almost invariably means more pay. However, using compensation as the only metric to validate lifelong employment implies that the goal is to earn more within the boundaries of society.

Only about one in four college graduates work within a field related to their major. Therefore, more than 70% of the American workforce earns limited compensation within an industry that was not their primary interest. Not surprisingly, this correlates to the same percentage of the workforce who wants to quit their job and start their own business.

BROAD OR DEEP?

Which one of your ancestors do you think would be more likely to climb a mountain successfully on their first attempt? Ancestor A is a climbing specialist schooled extensively and exclusively in climbing. Ancestor B is a generalist who recently learned how to climb after surviving all over the continent. Before you answer, consider this:

Despite the relative lack of available entrepreneurship programs, research shows that entrepreneurial-focused class content increases the likelihood of a student starting a business. It also increases their future wealth compared to entrepreneurs who lack formal education on the topic. Therefore, the expansion of entrepreneurship programs will eventually increase the number of businesses that are started and positively affect the success of those businesses.

Intuitively, this information might lead you to think about skipping a four-year degree and only studying entrepreneurship. That would be a mistake. Researchers have revealed that founders with diverse educational backgrounds are more likely to create successful companies.

---

6. Andrew Hacker, The Math Myth: And Other STEM Delusions, New York: The New Press, 2018.

Entrepreneurship revolves around agility and ever-changing variables. An entrepreneur needs to see the world through a different lens and engage in a fast-moving and dynamic marketplace. Therefore, would-be entrepreneurs should expose themselves to a broad mix of educational inputs and not just entrepreneurship content.[7]

The lessons learned in history, biology, and literature class empower entrepreneurs to face challenges, make decisions, and lead others. This empowerment leads to higher earnings. It is important to note that broad core studies alone do not positively impact entrepreneurs. But if the founder of a new business completed general core studies before a deep dive into creating a startup, the company is much more likely to be successful. Also, the founder's eventual wealth is usually much higher than their counterparts who lacked the core studies.

Education and earnings have a direct relationship. The more educated and experienced you are, the higher your earnings are likely to be as an employee. But as an entrepreneur, you need a broad, diverse educational foundation coupled with a depth of knowledge in your field and other entrepreneurship principles. A broad foundation alone or even specialization without a broad foundation is not enough.

To answer the original question, Ancestor B has a competitive advantage with general and diverse knowledge that serves as a solid foundation for new learning opportunities like climbing mountains. What if it snows? What if it rains? What food should be brought along for the climb? There is a lot to consider other than the climb itself. The baseline survival skills that early man possessed served as the springboard for geographic specialization. The same ability lies within your Boss Brain.

WHY DOES THIS MATTER?

There are thousands of ways to manipulate the stats for or against following the path that society prescribes. In the end, there is no doubt that a college degree increases the likelihood of obtaining a higher-paying job. It definitely does. That is not the problem. The problem is that our system tells you to follow your unique dream and then provides a single path

---

7. Dev K. Dutta, et al, "Fostering Entrepreneurship: Impact of Specialization and Diversity in Education," International Entrepreneurship and Management Journal, 7, 163-179. 10.1007/s11365-010-0151-2.

that supposedly leads to every destination. Broad core curriculum creates generalists. In the world of middle management, generalists prevail.

How can an entrepreneur follow the same path that every traditional employee follows and expect to end up self-employed? A comprehensive core curriculum will not make you the specialist that entrepreneurship requires. And being a specialist without more general knowledge is a liability in today's fast-moving and evolving marketplace.

At some point, entrepreneurs must build their own roads.

Your Boss Brain is a generalist with a preference for specialization. It empowered your ancestors to adapt and thrive in every climate, every elevation, every topography. But a baseline of skills was required before that specialization could occur. An aborigine of Australia might not need to know how to ice fish, but crafting a pole and tying a hook to a line are invaluable skills. An Inuit father doesn't teach his children to hunt with blowguns, but stalking is a critical part of hunting the world over. A business owner might not handle his accounting, but reading a profit & loss statement and knowing how to calculate your cost of goods are crucial.

Being an entrepreneur means committing to lifelong learning with ever-increasing levels of specialization. The current system purports that when your education is over, your career begins. The fact of the matter is that when college is over, your real training starts. Much of the knowledge you gain in school will inevitably be lost, but the skills that you acquire along the way are crucial to your success. Crossing a continent will better prepare you to climb its peaks.

KEY TAKEAWAYS

- Optimism and self-efficacy are not enough. To reshape your future, you must follow a different path and take unique action.
- Society sends conflicting messages of both individualism and assimilation.
- The American Dream has been distorted into a cultural narrative of consumerism that authors the life story of most Americans.
- Regardless of utility, everything that is customary was fabricated.

- The current education system leaves students ill-prepared to deal with the inevitable challenges of entrepreneurship.
- A college degree does not increase the likelihood of becoming a business owner.
- Within the context of education, ever-increasing specialization levels built on a broad foundation are the key to entrepreneurial success.

QUESTIONS TO ASK

- Am I willing to build my own road to reach my preferred destination?
- Am I working daily to become an expert in my field?
- How can I constantly expand the diversity of my baseline knowledge?
- What is my personal competitive advantage? What skills and knowledge do I bring to bear that others do not?

CHAPTER 4

THE FIRST PRIMARY INSTINCT

"TO MAKE ANY KIND OF PROGRESS, WE NEED TO
IMAGINE A DIFFERENT REALITY AND BELIEVE IT'S
POSSIBLE."
– TALI SHAROT, THE OPTIMISM BIAS

THE FIRST PRIMARY INSTINCT: BELIEF

The ruby-throated hummingbird is about three inches long and weighs about as much as a penny. Sometime during its evolution centuries ago, an ancestral ruby fattened herself up in the Yucatan Peninsula. But instead of migrating up through Mexico in late winter like all her fellow rubies, her instincts told her to take a different path. Lil' Ruby took a hard, right turn and set out across the Gulf of Mexico. After 18 hours of non-stop flying, she was in Florida.

Florida's flowers were already in bloom, so Lil' Ruby saved herself thousands of miles of migration. She crossed more than 500 miles of open ocean without resting, eating, or drinking and was rewarded handsomely for her efforts. She had her nest built before her sisters had even made it to Texas. Her trip required more than self-sacrifice and endurance. Her journey also required belief.

Before she launched herself from her perch, she had to believe three things: first, she had to believe that a better future awaited her on the

You were born into a relatively comfortable world that has lulled you into a compromised existence and bribed you with predictable adequacy.

other side of the Gulf. Second, she had to believe in her ability to traverse the open ocean. And third, she had to believe that taking action would improve her future. Today, thousands of rubies arrive in Florida every February because of her belief. She shaped the future, not just for herself but for her entire species. That is her legacy.

Every species on the planet wants to do two things: survive and procreate. Both plants and animals have this in common. Everything that lives shares these instincts. Some grow thorns to increase their chances of survival, while others fly over 500 miles of open ocean to nest and mate early. For every species throughout history, these two instincts were enough—that is, every species but one.

At some point in human history, one of our ancestors took a hard, right turn. She was fed up with merely surviving and procreating. She wanted her offspring to have a better life in a better place. But for her to leave the safety and security of the cave, she also had to believe three things, just like Lil' Ruby. She had to believe that a better future was possible. She had to believe in her ability to make that future a reality. However, optimism and self-efficacy were not enough. Change required action.

THE FIRST COMPONENT OF BELIEF: OPTIMISM

Optimism is the first component of the Primary Instinct of Belief. The world often associates optimism with naiveté, as if glasses are never half full, only half empty. However, to you and your Boss Brain, optimism is empowering. It is the ignition switch on the engine of your advancement.

Without optimism, mankind might have accepted caves and spears as the apex of existence. Complacency would have set in the moment our needs were consistently met. Instead of innovating and adapting, we would have built walls around our adequacy. With no ability to envision a better life, we would have accepted that our current existence was the only possible fate.

Here is the entrepreneurial enigma that has resulted from our collective rejection of optimism: *society has improved at the expense of individual fulfillment.* As an entrepreneur who feels stuck in traditional employment, you have sacrificed your optimism in exchange for the certainty of society's collective rise. You have been tricked into believing that the two ideas are mutually exclusive and that somehow pursuing your unique vision of the future is selfish and unrealistic. Nothing could be further from the truth. Adequacy is a metric of survival, and survival is not enough for you on an instinctive level. That's not selfish; it is the very spirit that brought on our success as a species.

You were born into a relatively comfortable world that has lulled you into a compromised existence and bribed you with predictable adequacy. That comfort has caged you and millions of other entrepreneurs in a prison of your own design. You have built walls around yourself and feel trapped and stagnant, even as the outside world continues to advance.

Fortunately, all the walls you built can be deconstructed. The barriers that stand between you and self-employment can be dismantled. To do that, you must use the same power that first inspired their construction: the power to envision a better future beyond your current line of sight—the power of optimism.

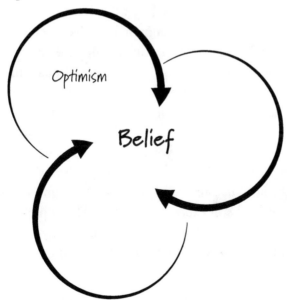

Optimism is the first component of the Primary Instinct of Belief

WAYS TO NURTURE YOUR INHERENT OPTIMISM

- Reject the need for absolute certainty and instead look for ways to maximize every opportunity.
- Just like your ancestors, think of relative comfort as a steppingstone, not a destination.
- Remember that predictable adequacy will not be adequate forever. Building walls around your present circumstances will inevitably limit your future rewards.
- Think of the future as a tangible product of your optimism. It isn't just a dream; it's a self-fulfilling prophecy.

THE SECOND COMPONENT OF BELIEF: SELF-EFFICACY

Self-efficacy is the second component of the Primary Instinct of Belief. Usually, the word describes a person that is resourceful and effective. But to the Boss Brain, self-efficacy is so much more than that. It is the gear shift on the engine that drives your advancement.

Self-efficacy is the result of layers of identity—not just who you think you are but also *what* you are at a more primal level. Without it, your actions are driven only by custom and by your environment. If you lack self-efficacy, you become paralyzed.

You and every other aspiring entrepreneur live in an increasingly competitive and socially relative environment. But the pressure to conform with and rise above those around you is a social quagmire. Your status is now measured against your peers and not against your true potential. Therefore, you have been absorbed into and become a product of your environment. Without self-efficacy, you will remain stuck somewhere between *what* you are and *who* you are expected to be.

If you want to move forward and make tomorrow better than today, you have to believe in your ability to do so. You cannot simultaneously restrain yourself and still expect to advance. The apprehension you feel emerges from your environment, but the confidence you feel comes from the inside. In this sense, self-efficacy isn't something you gain, it's something you unleash.

Fortunately, you can escape, reengineer, and even transcend your environment. But to do so, you must realize that the mistrust you have in your competence is self-limiting. If you can envision a better future but don't trust in yourself to get there, you'll never act. You're limited by your insecurities, not by the world around you.

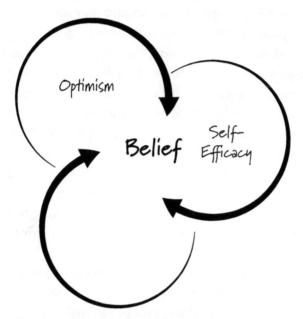

Self-efficacy is the second component of the Primary Instinct of Belief

WAYS TO NURTURE YOUR SELF-EFFICACY

- Practice recognizing what drives and motivates you beyond monetary gain.
- Seriously vet opportunities even when they seem out of reach or are inconsistent with who you think you are.
- Strip away your external identity and perception of self. Eliminating that lens will change your entire perspective on what you are and are not capable of.
- Trust in your adaptability and resourcefulness. That is what turns your optimism into action.

THE THIRD COMPONENT OF BELIEF: ACTION

Action is the last component of the Primary Instinct of Belief. Ordinarily, we use the word *action* to describe high-intensity movies and sports. If your optimism is the ignition switch and your self-efficacy is the gear shift, your actions are the gas pedal.

Most of the things you do are not actions; they are reactions. Too often, aspiring entrepreneurs are confused by the conflicting messages of American culture and get stuck. Or worse, they buy into the wrong definition of the American Dream . . . literally. After following the single path that society laid out, they soon find themselves chained to obligation. Without the specialization that entrepreneurship requires, decades pass before they have the expertise and the resources to initiate purposeful actions.

As an entrepreneur, you must take purposeful and self-initiated action. That's how you reveal previously hidden opportunities. There are no hidden opportunities on the same road that everyone travels. It was built as a reaction to the needs of employers. Following that road isn't a self-initiated action. It's a reaction. You can't expect to arrive in a different place by following that road.

When you discard your social identity and cut your path, you force your environment and all those within it to react to *you,* not the other way around. Their reaction to you creates external momentum, and you advance on the power of their efforts. Your subsequent momentum will then fuel your continued optimism. That's how belief is maintained: your self-efficacy converts your optimism into action.

Thankfully, initiating action is easy when you are optimistic and trust your abilities. And it is made even easier by the fact that the first steps are always the smallest. There is no magic. It is simply a decision. Will I convert my optimism to action and take the first step, or will I remain exactly where I am forever?

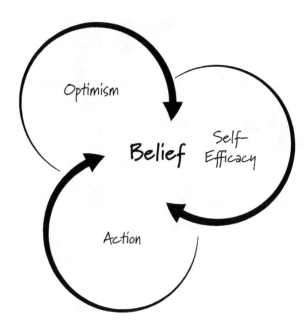

Action is the third component of the Primary Instinct of Belief

WAYS TO CONVERT YOUR OPTIMISM AND SELF-EFFICACY INTO ACTION

- Consciously question the legitimacy of cautionary tales about business ownership, especially from people who do not own their own business.
- Study personal finance and develop a realistic budget, including a short and long-term plan. This costs you nothing and is an easy first step.
- Embrace the fact that college is essential for the most part. However, the broad, core curriculum is only half the battle.
- You must become an expert in your field. Know your preferred industry better than anyone else: its history, current status, and future.

TRUE BELIEF

Optimism, self-efficacy, and action maintain the First Primary Instinct: Belief. Every action you take, no matter how small, was born of belief.

We often associate the word with larger, more philosophical concerns like religion and spirituality, but belief silently operates in the background of our lives all day.

Whether it is taking people at their word or proceeding through a green light, you believe in an expected outcome and govern yourself accordingly. You might not be willing to take a person at their word or proceed through a green light without looking both ways. And that just proves that your actions reveal what and when you truly believe.

Without actions that teach you something, the loop is broken, and belief fades. Optimism and self-efficacy are useless without action. You can have either or both, but unless you take actions that shape the future, your belief will wane and eventually disappear. Regardless of the outcome, every time you try something new, you learn something. The lessons you learn fuel your optimism because you now have a new approach or a new idea to try. That is how optimism is reignited, and the cycle is perpetuated.

To maintain true belief, all three components are required.

- You can be optimistic without having self-efficacy.
- You can be optimistic and trust in your abilities without ever taking action.
- You reshape your future only when your self-efficacy converts your optimism into action.

BEGINNING TO BELIEVE

In the final scene of the 1999 sci-fi blockbuster *The Matrix*, Neo decides to stand and face the evil, assimilation-seeking Agent Smith. His fellow rebel, Trinity, turns to Morpheus and asks, "What is he doing?" To which Morpheus responds, "He's beginning to believe." This seven-second scene launched 1000 memes of folks failing in a variety of ways. But it also begs an important question. When a person is short on evidence to support a belief, how do they begin to believe?

Every successful business was started by someone who converted their vision and self-confidence into action. But many would-entrepreneurs do not believe in their abilities. The solution to this problem comes in two parts.

Most of us are not incredibly self-aware; we do not really know ourselves. When self-reporting on what influences us and how we make decisions, we are infamously unreliable. We are almost always wrong about matters of self. If we are often mysteries to one another, then we are frequently mysteries to ourselves.

The first part of the solution is to view our unreliable answers as evidence of how we see ourselves. Let's say the question is, "Do you believe in your ability to make the future a better place for yourself and others?" and someone answers, "No." For the vast majority of us, we do not answer based on evidence. Instead, we answer no because we see ourselves as the kind of person who would not believe. Unreliable answers are self-reinforcement. They work to perpetuate our self-image and assert our identity.

The second part of the solution is to abandon any attempt to change what you believe about yourself. The end goal of belief is action. So instead of trying to improve your self-perception, focus on changing your behavior. This is a much more tangible way to approach the problem.

When we think about changing our self-image, we tend to think about knowing ourselves. But when we think about changing behavior, we focus on actions. As it turns out, having an accurate perception of ourselves changes nothing about how we behave. Decades of research prove that information alone does not change behavior.

The age-old adage that belief drives action is only correct if you already believe. For everyone else, beliefs are reverse engineered. We build our identities around what we and others like us do. As such, we will only construct a different identity after we start doing things differently.

For a non-believer, belief doesn't come first; action comes first. Taking consistent action inspires you to construct a whole new story about yourself. And that new person—who takes consistent action to reshape her future into a better place—is much more likely to believe in her abilities, just like Lil' Ruby.

CHAPTER 5

IT'S NOT MY FAULT

"THE BLAME DIMINISHES AS THE GUILT INCREASES."
—JOHANN FRIEDRICH VON SCHILLER

The world is chaotic. It has always been chaotic. But now, more than ever before, we are inundated with information proving just how chaotic the world really is. We see notifications about it on our phones when we wake. We hear about it on the radio during our morning commute. We see chaos on our news feeds. Many of the worst and most egregious symptoms of this chaos are pipelined directly into our inbox. As a result, it is easy to believe the world is spinning out of our control. Add in the exponential complexities of maintaining a career, and you've got a recipe for pure chaos.

Your twenty-first-century life may appear complicated compared to historical standards. Still, it is built on systems, beliefs, and ideologies that precede recorded history. Your modern-day, 280-character life is the apex of a biological, psychological, and societal pyramid whose construction began two hundred millennia ago. In today's terms, we have loaded a complicated operating system onto antiquated hardware. As a result, our brains struggle to load all the information and consistently look for solutions that require the least amount of memory.

Nothing requires less memory than giving up control.

Evolution wired the Boss Brain to take control and never quit. Quitting meant death. Therefore, nature selected quitters for extinction.

Then a strange thing happened. The Boss Brain unknowingly gave up control in exchange for predictability. It was a subtle shift at the time but eventually yielded painful unintended consequences. Although, that trade didn't remove the instinct to take control. Therefore, each day, the Boss Brain had to fight against its inherent drive for independence and freedom. Each day it endured the shame and humiliation of quitting. The best way to accept this fate and still believe in its abilities—its self-efficacy—was to blame something else.

Ask would-be entrepreneurs why they aren't doing what they want to do, and they will likely give you one of two answers. They will either claim that they do not have enough time to pursue that dream or say that they are prevented by uncontrollable circumstances. Most commonly, they point to elective personal projects and other imaginary hurdles that are not related in any way to their dream of business ownership—finishing their degree, remodeling their house, waiting until the kids graduate, etc. None of these are actual barriers to entrepreneurship, especially considering the funding and time that Americans have available to them.

America offers the most extensive entrepreneurship funding programs in the world. Yet, the U.S. self-employment percentage still ranked dead last among industrialized countries in 2018.[1] And despite the commonly held notion that there aren't enough hours in the day, the U.S. ranks 19th in the world for available leisure time at just under five hours a day. The average American watches TV for three of those hours.[2]

The problem isn't a lack of time or money. The problem is that we want to *believe* the lies we tell ourselves to avoid accountability.

> *The problem isn't a lack of time or money. The problem is that we want to believe the lies we tell ourselves to avoid accountability.*

---

1. "Self-employment rate (indicator)," OECD iLibrary viewed at https://www.oecd-ilibrary.org/employment/self-employment-rate/indicator/english_fb58715e-en.

2. Joyce Chepkemoi, "OECD Countries That Spent the Most Time on Leisure Activities," viewed at https://stats.oecd.org/Index.aspx?DataSetCode=BLI

SHOCKINGLY STRESSFUL

In 1958, Joseph Brady published the results of a study with two sets of monkeys. Both sets of monkeys were placed in restraining chairs and given electric shocks every 20 seconds for six hours on and six hours off each day for 23 days.

The first set of monkeys had no power to eliminate or prevent the shocks. They had no control over their situation and simply had to endure the pain. However, the second set had access to a lever, which, if pressed within 20 seconds, would prevent the electric jolt from occurring.

The results were counterintuitive. You might expect that the monkeys who could not prevent the shocks would go insane. The opposite occurred. Many of the monkeys with the ability to prevent their shocks died from perforated ulcers. The ulcers were a by-product of the stress associated with having full control over what they had to endure.

Amazingly, none of the monkeys in the first set ever developed ulcers. They just had to sit there and endure the pain. They had no control over their situation. They accepted their fate and were less stressed even though the shocks continued.

The conflict between optimism and uncertainty has spawned a litany of self-deceptions. None are quite so jaw-dropping as the modern brain's preference for giving up control and just enduring the shocks.

In today's world, we are expected to attach ourselves in ways that force us to endure these metaphorical shocks. Like everyone else, most would-be entrepreneurs go to school, get a job, and buy a house to create a safe, predictable life. Then they point to their workload, their mortgage, and their obligations as the reasons they can't pursue self-employment. They aren't just complicit in the destruction of their dreams; they take an active role. But still, they refuse to accept any blame.

Assigning blame to something or someone other than yourself is a nifty way to protect your self-perception. Ceding control helps you remain confident, especially when you assign it to items that bolster your stature in the community.

HIGHER EDUCATION AND LOWER LEVELS OF CONTROL

Experts long believed that as countries develop economically, people live longer lives. Greater access to wealth means more healthcare and better food. That assumption might lead you to think that citizens of oil-rich Equatorial Guinea would live longer on average than citizens of Cuba, which is very poor. The opposite is true.

Longevity and education are much more closely correlated than longevity and wealth. There is a direct relationship between education and life expectancy. That is why Cubans have a higher life expectancy than Americans, while people in Equatorial Guinea rarely live past 60. Cuba doesn't have rich oil reserves, but it does have a 97% literacy rate, two points higher than Equatorial Guinea.

Generally speaking, higher levels of education usually mean lower mortality rates. Ordinarily, with each standard deviation increase in education (such as from high school to an associate degree), mortality risk decreases by 17%. Economic disadvantages often go hand in hand with less education, which usually translates to shorter lives. But an exception to this rule exists. Sometimes people with PhDs are actually at *higher* risk of dying than others who are less educated. A recent study set out to determine if control could account for these differences.

Researchers measured the "control beliefs" of 6,000 people between the ages of 25 and 75. The subjects responded to how much they agreed with statements concerning their "personal mastery" and "perceived constraints." The statements included, "I can do just about anything I set my mind to" and "what happens in my life is beyond my control." The results showed the power of feeling in control. They also revealed how a sense of control interacts with education levels.

Among the less educated, those with a stronger sense of control rated their health better and smoked less than those who felt less in control. A stronger sense of control over life reduced the mortality rate risk by 13%. However, feeling in control didn't help much at higher education levels.[3]

The research suggests that the mental feeling of having control of your life creates a kind of physical resilience. Undesirable circumstances,

---

3. Anne E. Barrett & Erica L. Toothman, "Explaining age differences in women's emotional well-being: The role of subjective experiences of aging," Journal of Women & Aging, 28:4, 285-296.

coupled with a sense of being powerless to change things, could wear on a person's health over time. Feeling powerless to change your situation affects a person's inclination to exercise and refrain from smoking or other bad habits.

However, if your circumstances are undesirable and you feel empowered to change them, your body responds positively to that feeling of empowerment. Conversely, if you are not in an undesirable situation, a sense of control was inconsequential. This is an interesting point because increases in quality of life indicators reduce entrepreneurship. The more comfortable you are, the less likely you are to seek control.

> *The more comfortable you are, the less likely you are to seek control*

Despite the ulcer-inducing stress of control in Brady's monkeys, feeling empowered to change a bad situation is good for your health. The difference is that the obligation was thrust upon Brady's monkeys; they didn't choose to be caged and shocked. If their cages didn't have locks and offered a reward for pulling the lever, they could have chosen to risk the shock to gain a reward. But that is not how the study was structured. In metaphorical terms, they were controlled by the stick, not motivated by a carrot. It's the difference between leaving a job to be your own boss and being fired unexpectedly. It is the feeling of being the master of your fate rather than giving up control to avoid accountability.

Aspiring entrepreneurs choose the stick over the carrot and then blame the stick. They willingly cage themselves and then pretend like their cages have locks.

PARKINSON'S LAW

Think about your life and what or who controlled it as you aged. When were you in charge of your own life? If you gave up control over your own life, when did that happen? Who did you give authority to? It sounds like an easy question, but some thought on the subject might inspire more debate than you first think.

Most employees are told when to arrive for work, when to leave for lunch, and when to go home. Most of us aren't allowed to choose our schedule. We put in the time required by our employer. Our evenings are usually short and filled with laundry, cooking dinner, and doing the dishes. Once you are a parent, there's precious little time after the kids have their baths and get to bed. At that point, you are likely too tired to focus anyway.

To make matters worse, your weekends are probably filled with yard work, housework, and grocery shopping. With so much on your to-do list, it's tempting to think that you've already maxed out your bandwidth and can't produce more. Research suggests you can produce more and that your perception of being maxed out is related more to control than it is related to time or ability.

A recent study showed that employees were 10% more productive when empowered to adjust and control their environment in small ways. The study was originally designed to examine how comfort affects productivity. But it yielded unexpected results. Subjects who were offered dimmer switches for their lights self-reported higher levels of employee satisfaction and increased productivity levels.[4] The study showed that you are more productive when you feel that you have control over your environment.

Like the feeding grounds of the elephants in Chapter 2, productivity increases when we manufacture our environment. The people in the study didn't have to tear down trees or dig holes in the ground. In fact, they didn't have to make changes at all. They just had to *feel* empowered to do so if they wanted to. Installing dimmer switches generated a 10% increase in productivity. Imagine the returns that a more significant feeling of empowerment would yield.

We create the individual environments where we live. Then, after manufacturing our surroundings, we become a slave to them. Nearly all the tasks that fill our days are within our control to change or eliminate. The problem is that we have woven these cultural norms into our life story, and, therefore, see them as an indispensable part of life.

Cyril Parkinson captured this phenomenon in an essay published in 1955. "Work expands so as to fill the time allotted for its completion."[5]

---

4. Barry P. Haynes, "The impact of office comfort on productivity," Journal of Facilities Management, February 22, 2008.

5. C. Northcote Parkinson and Osbert Lancaster, Parkinson's Law, London: Penguin, 2002.

Parkinson was referring to the growth of bureaucracy in an organiza-
tion. Governmental and corporate growth continues even when all other
variables stay the same. The same is true for people. We set up processes
to maintain our lives then cede control to the very systems we created.

We pass our own little acts of Congress and then complain about all
the red tape.

IN THE MOMENT

More evidence for untapped bandwidth comes from the biological
stopwatch in your brain. In 2012, researchers published the results from
experiments examining the consequences of awe-filled experiences. The
participants in these experiments engaged in awe-inspiring activities like
interacting with huge animals or watching waterfalls. Compared to participants who completed more mundane activities, participants in the
awe conditions reported feeling time pass more slowly.[6]

The findings suggest that awe causes people to feel more present or
"in the moment." That causes them to perceive time as more abundant.
The same mechanisms cause time to pass more slowly when stuck in an
uncomfortable situation, as you are very aware of the moment and want
out. It doesn't matter whether you are getting a root canal or bottle-
feeding a baby panda at sunset. Either way, you are in the moment, and
time passes more slowly.

However, when you hop from one menial, uninspiring task to another all day, time flies. There are no awe-filled moments. When cooking
breakfast, you are thinking about getting the kids to school. When doing
laundry, you are thinking about paying bills. Your mind is always somewhere else. This phenomenon often occurs when driving. The route is
so familiar, so uninspiring, that we find ourselves pulling into the garage
and cannot remember making the drive.

With no perceived control over your environment and no awe-filled
moments on your to-do list, the days feel short and less productive. The
truth is, you definitely have more bandwidth when very little of your day
requires focused attention. It's not that you are overwhelmed; it's that

---

6. Joe Dawson and Scott Sleek, "The Fluidity of Time: Scientists Uncover How Emotions Alter Time
Perception," APS Observer, 2018.

the modern brain has given over control of your life to a ceaseless flow of uninspiring, unproductive tasks.

LOW MOTIVATION AND HIGH SELF-PERCEPTION

Right now, there is a battle raging between your motivation and your self-perception. Even though self-efficacy is a crucial element in the cycle of maintaining belief, it must be balanced with a willingness to fail and learn from those failures. Being in control means accepting responsibility for making things right when they go wrong, no matter who or what is to blame. If your self-perception is so fragile that you cannot endure a setback, you avoid failure to avoid accountability.

In 1985, the American psychologist Bernard Weiner revealed how this battle began. He developed a theory that focuses on achievement. Specifically, Weiner's theory uncovered the factors affecting where we place credit or blame for our accomplishments and failures. Weiner named these factors attributions. Attribution theory explains how we select and construct explanations for life events.

During an interview in 1996, Weiner said that "certain attributions are maladaptive in that they are likely to reduce achievement strivings." We usually assign the failure of others to internal attributions like low ability or effort. Simultaneously, we tend to attribute our failures to external attributions, like jobs and obligations. This makes us feel superior to others and warm and fuzzy inside. "Bob is always late. He has poor time management skills. However, I don't have poor time management skills—the train made me late."

Welcome to the reality that your lack of persistence is tied to the importance of your self-perception.

Would-be entrepreneurs who have given up control of their lives resort to telling themselves lies that serve their emotional insecurities. They attribute their inaction to external circumstances of their design and then claim that design is outside of their control.

Welcome to the reality that your lack of persistence is tied to the importance of your self-perception. "Maladaptive in that they are likely to reduce achievement strivings" is just a nice way of saying that to take personal responsibility for complacency and inaction might damage your precious ego.

The good news is that Dr. Weiner revealed how one thing could change all this: persistence.

Dr. Weiner's research showed that the longer our efforts persist, the more proficient we become at a particular task. He also revealed that higher proficiency makes tasks feel easier and produces higher expectations of future success. Tie those two together. Persistence results in greater ability, and greater ability results in higher expectations of success and lower perception of difficulty.

In short, the harder you work at something, the easier it becomes. And the longer you work at it, the more likely you are to succeed. But without persistent effort, everything feels harder than it actually is.

PREDICTING THE FUTURE

Tell me about yourself. It's an open-ended request. To answer, you can pick and choose whatever information you deem relevant based on the situation. Organizing the past into a personal narrative is how we make sense of life's chaos. Your life story is determined by how you frame critical moments that made you who you are and explain how you got to a particular place in time.

However, your story is more than a trail that you left behind; in your mind, it is also a roadmap to the future. We try to predict the future all the time. Our need for predictability motivates us to use our past narratives like a crystal ball. But to predict the future, our storyline must be unified, clear, and straight.

There is evidence that suggests that having a linear, well-defined life story is psychologically better for you. Why? Because it allows you to predict what will happen next.[7] We rearrange events in the past into a storyboard that explains the present and predicts the future. Research supports the mental link between the past and the future; the same regions of the brain that control memory light up when people imagine

---

7. K.C. McLean, et al "The Empirical Structure of Narrative Identity: The Initial Big Three," Journal of Personality and Social Psychology, 119(4), 920–944. https://doi.org/10.1037/pspp0000247.

an event that hasn't happened yet. This is one of the reasons why people with severe amnesia have trouble imagining the future.

When you build a personal narrative, you pull moments and events from the chaos of your life to create a central theme, to create a unified story. As one researcher put it, "The future is never a direct replica of the past. So, we need to be able to take pieces of things that have happened to us and reconfigure them into possible futures."

A problem occurs, though, when past events don't fit neatly into the storyline. What do you do with all those events and experiences that don't support the story you are telling yourself? All those dead ends and wrong turns make the future feel uncertain, and uncertainty is uncomfortable. Instead of keeping those events and moments and learning from them, it is easier to drop them and find other moments that confirm the narrative.

"If you're planning to be a doctor, and you're a 25-year-old starting medical school, and you have expectations about what the next five to 10 years are going to be like, you've probably construed a narrative from your past that helps you understand how you got to this point," says one researcher. "Then, you get into med school, and you hate it, and you drop out. You probably, at the same time, are going to change your past. You rewrite the history."

Nothing is more powerful or more delusional than rewriting history. We pick and choose past events and experiences, give them power over how we view our current circumstances, and paste them into a vision of the future. All your memories and life moments are up for grabs as you construct a narrative for yourself like a character in a play. But in truth, you are both playwright and protagonist, both director and star. We rewrite the first act while living the second, and we allow that delusion to author the third.

WHY DOES THIS MATTER?

We all suffer from the same self-serving biases. We feed into the idea that our failures and inaction are attributed to some external cause, something outside our control. We claim that it isn't our fault. Blaming something else makes us feel better about ourselves, but it also limits our persistence.

We foolishly begin to believe the lies we tell ourselves. As a result, we feel powerless. Then finally, we accept our fate and just endure the shocks.

The Boss Brain craves responsibility and takes control. It rejects any suggestion that it is not in full control of its destiny. It knows that any attempt to blame something else is self-deception. Even if circumstances require assigning control temporarily, the Boss Brain makes that choice voluntarily. Just like temporary boundaries, it can choose to lift those limitations and regain control.

Those who refuse to accept complete and total responsibility for their lives rarely succeed as entrepreneurs. They may retain their optimism. They may even overcome their need for certainty. But without a willingness to accept that they are in full control of their business, they will likely fail. Why? Because feeling powerless leads to complacency. Anyone who believes that they are not in control is less likely to change the circumstances and more likely to quit rather than continue searching for a solution. They place blame everywhere but on themselves as they construct and revise narratives of vindication.

The fax machine was out of paper, so we didn't receive your order. An employee called in sick, and we won't meet your deadline. The local permitting office closes at 4 P.M., so we can't break ground tomorrow. Your overnight package won't be there by 10 A.M. as promised because our delivery truck got stuck in traffic. I don't have poor time management; the train made me late.

Pretending that something or someone has power over your life and the outcome of your efforts is the path to mediocrity. The hard truth is, when you accept no blame for your current circumstances, you are giving the past control over your future.

KEY POINTS

- Anything that you think controls you only does so because you allow it.
- Feeling empowered and having a sense of control positively affects your health and satisfaction with life.
- We pretend that we don't have control to excuse our lack of effort and maintain a positive perception of ourselves.

- We choose our obligations and then blame them for obligating us.
- Diligence and resilience increase proficiency which increases the likelihood of success.

QUESTIONS TO ASK

- What and who have I given power over me, and how might I recapture that control?
- Do I believe I control the outcome of unforeseen challenges, or do I relent as if fate is in control?
- Am I willing to accept total and singular responsibility for a failure to act and my current conditions?
- Would I rather pretend I don't have control to avoid taking responsibility?

CHAPTER 6

I COULD IF I WANTED TO

"SELF-DECEPTION FOOLS ALL OF THE PEOPLE
ALL OF THE TIME."
—MARTY RUBIN

In 1876, a three-year-old boy named George fell out of a tree near his home in Ontario. George suffered a blood clot in his brain, lost the use of his right arm, and was paralyzed from the waist down. Doctors said that he would likely never walk again.

George refused to accept that diagnosis. He turned to exercise to overcome his injuries. Seven years after his fall, George walked, and two years later, he was fully mobile. At the age of 12, George's redemption story would have been impressive even if it ended there. But George was not done writing his life story.

George continued training and fell in love with distance running. He attended the University of Toronto and joined the track team. He dominated the half-mile and mile runs at meets in Canada and the United States. He also set the university's one-mile record in 1892, clocking a time that was only a few seconds off the then world record.

George won 17 national titles in the United States, seven in Canada, and one in the United Kingdom. He won the U.S. one-mile championship six times, the two-mile steeplechase seven times, the cross country twice, the five-mile run, and the ten-mile run. Still missing the use of his right arm, he introduced ice hockey to Philadelphia and captained the first team there. George's life story could have ended there, but he wasn't finished.

George went on to compete in the 1900 Summer Olympics in Paris. He contracted an intestinal virus the day before the competition and still won a bronze medal in the 400m hurdles. Less than an hour later, George won the gold medal and set a world record in the 2500m steeplechase. He even placed fifth in the 4000m steeplechase the next day while severely dehydrated from his stomach bug. George was the first Canadian and the first disabled athlete to win an Olympic gold medal.

One might say that Dr. George Washington Orton was simply a gifted natural athlete who overcame a terrible childhood accident. True enough, but during the time that he won 131 races, including 33 national and international championships, George also earned a master's degree and his PhD. He authored a series of books, was a member of the American Academy of Poets, and learned to speak nine languages.

The question is: did George achieve so much despite his challenges or because of them?

HARD WORK BEATS TALENT EVERY TIME

At birth, the human brain has no understanding of inherent ability. As a result, children attempt tasks with the mindset that success is inevitable if they work hard enough. Their diligence diminishes only when they are finally old enough to understand that each person is born with natural gifts. Once people think that talent is something they either have or don't have, failure becomes a litmus test for ability. Both the gifted and the non-gifted are affected.

> *The gifted and the non-gifted are two sides of the same coin. For both, the importance of their self-perception undermines their effort.*

The naturally gifted put forth less effort because their self-perception needs no validation. To them, working hard is something that others must do. Plus, confidence in their abilities would make failure much more difficult to accept.

Those who lack inherent gifts work less for the opposite reason. To them, working hard and failing would validate their inadequacy. The gifted and the non-gifted are two sides of the same coin. For both, the importance of their self-perception undermines their effort. But what if sustained effort did not validate the presence of natural ability? Instead, what if sustained effort is itself a skill that can be cultivated? Research on the psychology of success hints that this is indeed the case.

In 1998, Carol Dweck and Claudia Mueller published a study on how fifth graders tackle difficult test questions. One at a time, each student was taken out of their regular class and into a test room. They were asked to solve a set of moderately difficult problems. After four minutes, the student was told to stop working, and the researcher reviewed their answers. It was at this point that the real experiment began.

All of the students were told that they had done well. In some cases, that was their only feedback. Other times, however, the researcher offered additional praise for either the student's ability or effort. They would say something like, "wow, you are brilliant," or "wow, you worked hard on these." The only thing that differed was the feedback at this moment. Otherwise, the researchers treated everyone the same.

Amazingly, when the students were given new, more difficult problems, those who were previously praised for their hard work and effort scored higher than those praised only for their ability. Praising effort, not ability, motivated the students to work harder.

Praising ability is commonly thought to drive a person. But this study revealed that praise for intelligence reduced motivation compared to praise for effort. The fifth graders that were praised for intelligence cared more about performance than learning. After failure, they displayed less persistence and attributed their failure to lack of ability, not lack of effort.[1]

George Orton's accident occurred before he was old enough to display inherent athletic ability. During his recovery, his parents and doctors could only praise him for his hard work. When we praise people for hard work, they are inspired to take risks. They learn from their mistakes and move on. And while Orton was undoubtedly a gifted athlete, his

1. C. M. Mueller, & C. S. Dweck, "Praise for intelligence can undermine children's motivation and performance," Journal of Personality and Social Psychology, 75(1), 33–52.

accident removed the need to prove his natural talent, where any setback would seem like a failure. Instead, he was motivated by constant praise for his effort, not his ability. Ironically, had his accident never happened, he would have likely been praised for his abilities, which would have undermined his drive to compete.

At the end of the study, all the fifth graders were offered a choice. They could read about how to do better on the test next time, or they could see the other kids' test scores. The effort-praised kids were much more likely to choose the test improvement option. They chose the option that would teach them to get better. On the other hand, the ability-praised kids were much more likely to want to see how everyone else had performed. They chose the option that would validate their self-perception and feelings of superiority.

Greatness is not determined by your natural gifts; it is determined by your ability to sustain effort.

Natural gifts are relative. Effort is not. Orton could have stopped at three languages, 100 races, and a master's degree. That would have put him well above the average level of education and athletic ability, and he could have reveled in his exceptionalism. But that would have left him with unrealized potential. Instead, he sustained his efforts well into his life. He even played soccer in the Philadelphia league at the age of 50.

Greatness is not determined by your natural gifts; it is determined by your ability to sustain effort. And sustained effort is a skill that can be nurtured and grown.

LOVE THE PROCESS, NOT THE PRIZE

Entrepreneurship is often, if not always, humbling. Many variables are unpredictable. But that is precisely why sustained effort is a crucial element. No one is born with the innate ability to manage unpredictable variables. So, failure itself does not necessarily indicate a lack of talent. Everyone is born with the ability to adjust to challenges, revise their plans, and try again.

After just one statement praising their ability, the students in Dweck's study were more likely to choose easy tasks that taught them nothing new. When challenged, they gave up more quickly. They were more likely to lie about their results and were even more willing to cheat to get a good result. All this after just *one statement* from a researcher whom they had never met. Now imagine the effects of a lifetime of being told how talented you are.

Sadly, the problem extends well beyond fifth grade. Society responds to success by saying, "wow, that person is incredibly talented." We praise the pop star, the business mogul, and the Olympian for their abilities. The problem with that mentality is devastating to entrepreneurial efforts: ability is innate, permanent, and uncontrollable. Therefore, we believe that success is imbued at birth. Rather than test the limits of our potential, we choose the easiest route, the one that confirms what we want to believe, not the one that tells us the most about ourselves. We emphasize the prize rather than the process by which it was attained. The outcome is more important to us than the effort it required.

Praising for intelligence, talent, and other innate abilities teaches the brain to adopt what Dweck calls a "fixed mindset," where results measure skill. If I'm doing well, it means I'm good at this. If I'm not doing well, I must be bad at it. This binary view of ability implies that results are predetermined and that the process is irrelevant. We feel powerless to change the outcome and are then motivated to choose the route that makes us look most capable. And that choice is the last nail in the entrepreneurial coffin.

The most impressive people are the ones who achieve amazing results without appearing to put in much effort. That shows they must be talented. But starting your own business always requires a tremendous amount of effort. Society heralds hard work as the key ingredient for entrepreneurial success, but it also judges anyone who appears to work hard as having low natural ability. If you ask for help, work hard, and put in long hours, you reveal that you aren't an inherently talented entrepreneur. As long as everything is easy and you continue to do well, having a fixed mindset isn't a problem. In fact, it will probably make you feel good about yourself.

However, when you focus on your behavior and not on the outcome, you are forced to adopt a growth mindset. The way you act and the effort that you apply then determine your results. In contrast to permanent and unchanging abilities, behaviors and efforts are temporary. If you're not good at something, you need to temporarily change your behavior and try to get better. You are in control of your results because you are the one who chooses how to act and how much effort to put in.

> *When you focus on your behavior and not on the outcome, you are forced to adopt a growth mindset.*

REDEMPTION DOES NOT REQUIRE ABILITY

There is one situation where society does not judge you negatively for working hard—the redemption story. At some point, every person will face a challenging situation—where things stop being easy—and serious effort is required.

No one watched the movie *Cast Away* and remarked, "Tom Hanks must be really bad at being marooned on an island. It took him five years to escape, and he almost died in the process!" Quite the opposite. The entire story was one of sustained effort and his relentless drive to overcome the situation. His abilities had nothing to do with it. Only his effort mattered. And with love and life on the line, success meant redemption. Framing your efforts in the context of redemption means society will support you, not judge you.

By continuing to get better over time, you are doing what every person wants to do—you are exceeding society's expectations. Audience members would have been furious if Tom Hanks had died on his raft after leaving his island. That outcome would not have defined his effort, but it was still relevant because success meant redemption. In redemption stories, the most impressive people are not the ones who make it look easy. They are the ones who don't give up, who keep trying creative ideas until they figure out a way to make things work.

Also, when Tom Hanks saw the passing ship, he didn't just let them pass and focus on redemption by his actions alone. He waved them down; he asked for help. Asking for help isn't a bad thing in redemption stories. It is a sign that you believe someone can help you get better faster. That you can more quickly achieve your desired result.

Conversely, refusing help from others shows that you don't want to get better. It reinforces your positive self-perception. If you go it alone and succeed, then you can pat yourself on the back and take all the credit. If you go it alone and fail, then you can blame the fact that you never had any help. This is redemption in your eyes only, not in reality.

The entrepreneur who stands up to challenges and finds redemption through sheer will is loved and supported by all. Customers identify with the struggle, and their patronage pays homage to relentless effort. It is their opportunity to share in the glory of redemption.

EFFORT IS AN ART

It is often said that art is pain. As if creativity emerges only from strife. Van Gogh painted *The Starry Night* after a mental breakdown that resulted in him cutting off his left ear and voluntarily checking himself into an insane asylum. After the death of his wife and one of his daughters, John Milton went blind before dictating *Paradise Lost* to his remaining daughters. And Eric Clapton penned his hit song *Tears in Heaven* after the tragic death of his son.

Creation is often cathartic, and we have a strange fascination with art forged in grief. However, despite popular belief, most art isn't wrought from pain, and most technological advances do not spring from muses. Like art and all other professions, entrepreneurial innovation emerges through a commitment to a process and relentless effort.

It is easy to visit a gallery and forget that the paintings are the end products of an arduous process that extends well beyond creative inspiration. In their lines and swirls, paintings hold long nights, early mornings, frustration, and failure, along with enormous amounts of physical and logistical details. An iconic painting requires tireless effort.

In one interview, legendary painter, artist, and photographer Chuck Close discussed why work ethic within a process is more important than inspiration:

> Inspiration is for amateurs—the rest of us just show up
> and get to work. And the belief that things will grow out of
> the activity itself and that you will—through work—bump

into other possibilities and kick open other doors that you
would never have dreamt of if you were just sitting around
looking for a great 'art idea.' And the belief that process, in
a sense, is liberating and that you don't have to
reinvent the wheel every day.

As a child, Close suffered from a neuromuscular condition that often kept him out of school. He also suffered from dyslexia and prosopagnosia, a condition that prevented him from recognizing familiar faces. Despite—or perhaps because of—his challenges, Close showed up and got to work, regardless of his current level of motivation. His story could have ended when he suffered from a spinal artery collapse that left him paralyzed, but Close wasn't finished. He continued to paint.

The Russian composer Pyotr Ilyich Tchaikovsky knew Chuck's secret more than 150 years ago. Tchaikovsky once wrote this about his fellow composers, "If we wait for the mood, without endeavoring to meet it halfway, we easily become indolent and apathetic. We must be patient and believe that inspiration will come to those who can master their disinclination . . . This is why, despite great gifts, they accomplish so little." His gifted peers would throw up their hands and quit at the slightest difficulty, just like Dweck's fifth graders. On the other hand, Tchaikovsky and Close both cultivated creativity through tireless effort.

Close believes that results don't necessarily require inspiration. He says they emerge when a person backs himself into a corner where no one else's answers will fit. When you do that, you must work tirelessly to find solutions to the problem that you have set for yourself.

WHY DOES THIS MATTER?

In any new endeavor, failure at some level is guaranteed. Accept it, embrace it, learn from it, and get better. Failure is not an indictment of your ability or your intelligence. To view it as such will weaken your commitment. Remember, you can be committed to entrepreneurship, or you can be committed to your self-perception. You cannot be committed to both. The inevitable setbacks and unforeseen challenges of transitioning to self-employment prevent that from happening.

At age five, George Orton just wanted to walk again. At age 12, he did just that. But instead of focusing on the outcome, he focused on effort and fell in love with the process. His accident might have paralyzed his legs, but it also prevented him from being paralyzed by fear of inadequacy. With no baseline perception of ability, he could only try and try again.

By focusing on the process, Orton was constantly reminded that he had the power to change his results. Confirmation of inherent ability played no part in his determination. For him, shifting behavior and getting better was itself a motivator. He might have been a naturally gifted runner, but that was not what defined him. Hard work was his greatest talent.

Within every dream lies hope—hope that with hard work and relentless effort, we can get better and better until our ultimate goals are achieved. That's what motivates us to continue, even when things aren't going our way. Success is not the end of a process that starts at point A and ends at point B. It is the by-product of sustained effort in the face of adversity.

KEY POINTS

- Working within a process is the only way to accurately measure the results of your effort, revise your plans accordingly, and get better.
- Praising inherent ability reduces the willingness to expend effort and weakens your determination and resilience.
- Praising effort and strategy increases mental resilience and increases your determination.
- Motivation is sustained by reflection on growth and improvement, not on outcome.
- Natural ability is relative. Effort is not.

QUESTIONS TO ASK

- Do I consider myself to be inherently talented, and how does that affect my work ethic?
- Have I nurtured and developed my talents, or do I avoid improvement because I fear failure?

- Do I choose the easiest paths because they complement my self-image?
- Have I clearly defined a process that allows me to measure my results objectively and get better while advancing toward my eventual goal?

CHAPTER 7

IT'S NOT WORTH THE EFFORT

"PEOPLE PRETEND NOT TO LIKE GRAPES WHEN THE
VINES ARE TOO HIGH FOR THEM TO REACH."
—MARGUERITE DE NAVARRE

One of the most momentous events in American history lacked the support of half of the country. During America's race to the moon, public support for NASA rarely rose above 50%. Throughout the 1960s, Americans often ranked the Apollo program near the top of programs that should be cut from the federal budget. When Apollo 11 landed on the moon, only 53% of Americans agreed that the result justified the expense.

The problem arose when Russia publicly announced it did not intend to send a man to the moon. They claimed to be more interested in sending satellites and probes that did not risk human life. Radio Moscow even called America's Apollo 11 program "the fanatical squandering of wealth looted from the oppressed peoples of the developing world."

Americans living in a sluggish economy believed the resources were better spent elsewhere. More than half the country thought the U.S. government fabricated the race to the moon to garner public support for such massive spending. In 1964, *The New York Times* published an editorial that read, "There is still time to call off what has become a one-nation race." Senator J. William Fulbright publicly announced that "we are in a race not with the Russians, but with ourselves." And even iconic anchor Walter Cronkite proclaimed on the fifth anniversary of the moon landing that "the Russians were never in the race at all."

Twenty years after Americans walked on the moon, a group of aerospace engineers from the Massachusetts Institute of Technology took a tour of the engineering laboratory at the Moscow Aviation Institute. In a large hall filled with old spacecraft, an engineer named Ed Crawley saw something that looked like the American lunar module. When he asked about it, the Soviets replied that it was indeed the lander they intended to send to the moon.

It turns out the Soviets were in the race to the moon after all. They built a landing module but failed to design rockets that were reliable enough to get to the moon. To cover up their failures, they pretended like they didn't even want to go to the moon. It was a lie the world believed until 1989.

THE EFFORT PARADOX

One of the most immutable laws of nature is the law of energy conservation. Effort is costly. Whether you are a cheetah sprinting at 100km per hour or an entrepreneur trying to get your business off the ground, your mind is constantly calculating the value of the rewards your efforts will reap. In general, Mother Nature has instilled in us all an aversion to extreme effort and not just the physical kind. We also take mental shortcuts to avoid overthinking. Psychology has very few laws, but the law of least mental effort is one of them. If two options offer similar rewards, most organisms with a brain choose the option that requires the least effort. But new research suggests that choosing the easier route is only part of the story.

If two options offer similar rewards, most organisms with a brain choose the option that requires the least effort.

Obviously, our willingness to expend energy to pursue a reward will increase as the prize becomes more valuable. But psychological research conducted in 2018 reveals that hard work increases the perceived value of the rewards. It also showed how expended effort could itself be rewarding.[1]

If you travel to buy a gallon of milk, traditional economic models dictate that you should value that milk less than if it was delivered to your front door. Because your time and energy have value, they are factored into the calculations in your head. However, the opposite occurs. Early research mistakenly presumed that this phenomenon represented the perceived value of the milk, not the value of the effort to attain it. The gallon of milk is identical in both scenarios. Still, we consider the one that required more effort to obtain to be more valuable.

The 17th-century philosopher Montaigne captured the essence of this anomaly when he wrote, "The fear of the fall more fevers me than the fall itself. The game is not worth the candle." Montaigne was referring to gambling after dark when the winnings were rarely more than the cost of the candle that lit the gaming table. Candles were hard to come by in the 17th century. The average person would burn a candle only for a very good reason. If a candle was lit, the person who was least adept at accomplishing the task that required light would hold it for the person who was more skilled and could accomplish the task more quickly.

Two common metaphors were born of this scenario. First, something that is 'not worth the candle' requires too much effort relative to its value. And second, a person who 'can't hold a candle' to another is far less skilled.

WHY DOES RICE PLAY TEXAS?

On September 12, 1962, President John F. Kennedy kicked off the race to the moon during a speech at Rice University. He even set a deadline to get there. This aggressive goal would reveal if American ingenuity truly deserved its reputation. In front of a crowd of 40,000 at Rice's football stadium, Kennedy explained the effort paradox 56 years before university researchers:

> But why, some say, the Moon? Why choose this as our goal?
> And they may well ask, why climb the highest mountain?

---

1. M. Inzlicht, et al, "The Effort Paradox: Effort Is Both Costly and Valued," *Trends in Cognitive Sciences*, 22(4), 337–349. https://doi.org/10.1016/j.tics.2018.01.007.

Why, 35 years ago, fly the Atlantic? Why does Rice play
Texas? We choose to go to the Moon! We choose to go to
the Moon . . . We choose to go to the Moon in this decade
and do the other things, not because they are easy, but
because they are hard; because that goal will serve to
organize and measure the best of our energies
and skills . . .

Researchers need only look to our ancestors to validate the effort paradox. There was never an urgent need to leave the caves or climb mountains or traverse continents. Just like there was no pressing need for man to go to the moon. Today, most entrepreneurs have no urgent need to leave their jobs and start their own businesses. But their Boss Brain drives them to test the limits of their potential, or as President Kennedy put it, "organize and measure the best of (their) energies and skills."

With that speech, Kennedy tapped into the pioneering spirit of America. American exceptionalism has always been about choice, not necessity. Kennedy repeated the phrase "we choose to go to the Moon" three times in a row and then even conceded that space exploration wasn't essential. He intentionally emphasized the freedom all Americans have to choose their destiny rather than have it chosen for them.

From that day on, NASA's space program was a constant topic of discussion. However, the Soviets didn't publicly announce their efforts. They didn't even admit their program existed. When Kennedy met with Nikita Khrushchev in June 1961, Kennedy proposed making the moon landing a joint effort. Khrushchev did not accept his offer. Then, as Kennedy predicted, the U.S. reached the moon in 1969. The Soviets continued to publicly deny the existence of their moon program even though they continued their efforts into the early 1970s.

In December 1989, *The New York Times*—which previously called the Apollo program a one-nation race—ran a front-page headline that read, "Now, Soviets Acknowledge A Moon Race." A Soviet journalist responded to the breaking news by saying, "secrecy was necessary so that no one would overtake us, but later, when they did overtake us, we had to maintain secrecy so that no one knew that we had been overtaken."

Like many of us, when we face a seemingly insurmountable challenge, Russia pretended that putting a man on the moon was not worth the candle. But in truth, they simply couldn't hold a candle to American ingenuity and effort to do the same.

Russia feared failure, so they lied to the world. When aspiring entrepreneurs fear failure, they lie to themselves.

THE IKEA EFFECT AND THE VALUE OF PAIN

What item would you be willing to pay more for—a bowl that is stamped out of metal by a machine or a hand-carved bowl? Similarly, would you be more willing to spend your hard-earned money or money that you won playing the lottery? If you are like most people, you would pay more for the handmade bowl and be more likely to spend your lottery winnings.[2][3] Research has proven over and over that the more an item requires energy, by you or by someone else, the more value it is assigned.[4] A person who worked very hard to gain access to a sold-out concert will enjoy the show more than a person who received a free ticket. This is sometimes called the Ikea effect. Consumers assign more value to items that require their effort as well as money—not just money.[5]

The amazing value of effort isn't just something we assign in retrospect. New research suggests that value can also come from expected effort. Studies have shown that people contribute more to future charitable events that are painful or effortful.[6] Mud runs, 5Ks, and other physical events earn more donations than potlucks, raffles, and auctions. This phenomenon begs an important question: how do we learn to associate effort with value?

Greater effort usually brings greater rewards. Animals, including humans, often attempt difficult tasks because of their promised rewards.[7]

2. C.Y. Olivola, "When noble means hinder noble ends: the benefits and costs of a preference for martyrdom in altruism," The Science of Giving: Experimental Approaches to the Study of Charity (D.M. Oppenheimer and C.Y. Olivola, eds,), pp. 49–62, Taylor & Francis.

3. S. Muehlbacher S and E. Kirchler E "Origin of endowments in public good games: the impact of effort on contributions," Psychol. Econ 2, 59–67.

4. Leon Festinger, A Theory of Cognitive Dissonance, Stanford, Calif: Stanford University Press, 2009.

5. M. I. Norton, et al, "The IKEA effect: when labor leads to love," Psychol 22, 453–460.

6. C. Olivola and E. Shafir E, "The martyrdom effect: when pain and effort increase prosocial contributions," J. Behav. Decis. Mak 26, 91–105.

7. M. A. Apps, et al, "The role of cognitive effort in subjective reward devaluation and risky decision-making," Sci Rep. Nov 20, 2015; 5():16880.

Studying more brings a better grade. Training harder means a competitive advantage in sports. When high effort is consistently paired with high reward, over time, the effort itself becomes self-reinforcing. Like Pavlov's dogs salivating at the sound of a bell, tremendous effort signifies imminent reward.

Psychologists call this learned industriousness.[8] A lifetime of high rewards following maximum effort results in the effort itself having value. Learned industriousness is a hallmark of the Boss Brain. The higher the effort, the greater the perceived value of the reward. Combine this mentality with innate optimism, and you have a recipe for choosing to exert relentless effort toward difficult tasks. This is why self-employed people are more engaged, more satisfied, and happier with work than traditional employees.[9]

The higher the effort, the greater the perceived value of the reward.

But what if society's path deprived a person of a lifetime of high rewards after maximum effort? What if, within the confines of employment, even maximum effort failed to change a bad situation and yielded no increase in rewards? Eventually, you would come to believe that no amount of effort will make things better. At that point, you would have what psychologists call *learned helplessness.*

Learned helplessness is the opposite of self-efficacy. People with high levels of self-efficacy believe they have innate and direct control over the outcomes of a situation. On the other hand, those with learned helplessness believe that no action, no matter how strenuous, will change the outcome. They believe that they are powerless to change outcomes or escape painful situations, even when presented with chances to do so.[10] The researchers who first documented this used dogs to show that neither threats nor rewards motivated action once learned helplessness had taken over. Even other dogs demonstrating exactly how to escape

8. Eisenberger, "Learned industriousness," Psychol Rev. 1992 Apr; 99(2):248-67.

9. "Work-life 3.0: Understanding how we'll work next," Price Waterhouse Coopers viewed at https://www.pwc.com/us/en/industry/entertainment-media/publications/consumer-intelligence-series/assets/pwc-consumer-intellgience-series-future-of-work-june-2016.pdf.

10. Neil R. Carlson, Psychology: The Science of Behavior, Pearson Canada, 2014, 409.

the negative stimulus still did not motivate action among the dogs who believed they were powerless.

Some common symptoms of learned helplessness in people include low self-esteem, poor motivation, lack of effort, frustration, procrastination, and a refusal to ask for help. Like the Yale monkeys that stopped pressing buttons and Dweck's fifth-graders, those who believe they are powerless to change the outcome of their employment situation see no value in trying. To them, there is no reason to try. Threats from their boss only make them feel more powerless. When all around them, entrepreneurs show them exactly how to escape, they continue to endure what they feel is inescapable.

PROLONGED EFFORT OR TEMPORARY REWARDS

Most people set personal goals for themselves. Others have goals set for them by their employer or society in general. Losing weight and buying a house are both common goals that require unique steps to achieve. Once fulfilled, a person can then enjoy being thinner or relaxing in their own home. But the effort to achieve a temporary goal doesn't fundamentally change you. Research suggests that, for the most part, the rewards of goal setting succeed at only one thing: temporary compliance.

Temporary rewards do not produce lasting changes in attitudes and behavior. Even in the corporate world, temporary rewards, like punishment, have proven ineffective long-term motivators. Once you hit your goal weight, you stop dieting and regain the weight you lost. Once you own your own home, you stop penny-pinching and saving. People almost always revert to their old behaviors.

The negative effect that external incentives have on motivation is twofold. First, whoever gets the reward assumes that bribes are only offered for otherwise undesirable tasks, i.e., not worth the effort. In 1992, Professor Jonathan L. Freedman and his colleagues at the University of Toronto confirmed that the greater the incentive offered for doing an activity, the more negatively the activity is viewed.[11] Second, external incentives divert our attention to the attainment of the reward, not

---

11. Jonathan Freedman, et al, "Inferred Values and the Reverse-Incentive Effect in Induced Compliance," Journal of Personality and Social Psychology. 62. 357-368. 10.1037/0022-3514.62.3.357.

solving the problem. When externally incentivized, people perform worse on problems that require creative thinking. Researchers assumed that rewards would increase the quality of work, but their research revealed the opposite.

"People will do precisely what they are asked to do if the reward is significant," says Monroe J. Haegele, author, and proponent of incentive programs.[12] And therein lies the root of the problem. Neither the carrot nor the stick creates lasting change. People will adjust their behavior just enough to get a carrot or avoid a stick. During that time, they are less inclined to take risks and explore possibilities. They become more dutiful and less open to new ideas. But once those incentives are removed or achieved, they revert to their intrinsic motivation levels or innate baseline willingness to exert effort.

The desire to create a lasting legacy pulls us in one direction, short-term rewards pull us in another. Those who diet will often weigh themselves every day. They are focused on hitting their desired number, not on being healthy. Those who want to own their own home obsessively check their account balance. They are focused on their down payment, not on financial planning. People will even engage in unethical and illegal behavior to create the illusion of performance, as many public companies have done before publishing their earnings.

In the modern world, temporary rewards buy temporary compliance: work hard, and you'll earn your quarterly bonus; exercise often, and you'll lose weight before spring. Tell someone to do *this,* and you'll get *that* puts the focus on the reward at the expense of sustained effort. This binary cause-and-effect mentality has woven itself into American culture, and societal incentives have slowly eroded entrepreneurial efforts. Each

> *People will adjust their behavior just enough to get a carrot or avoid a stick. During that time, they are less inclined to take risks and explore possibilities.*

---

12. Monroe J. Haegele "The New Performance Measures," in The Compensation Handbook, Third Edition, edited by Milton L. Rock and Lance A. Berger (New York: McGraw-Hill, 1991).

year more and more people lower their goals to achieve the quickest and easiest rewards for their efforts.

Our national rewards-based mindset is rooted in the belief that external incentives drive motivation. But that mindset is a façade. Extrinsic motivators do not alter our attitudes. They do not create an enduring commitment to an ideal or a cause. External incentives don't change who we are. They simply temporarily change what we do.

WHY DOES THIS MATTER?

The power of learned industriousness is hardwired into your Boss Brain. Those who worked harder reaped greater rewards . . . period. Of course, good and bad luck can play a role in singular circumstances, but the value of consistently choosing that which is difficult compounds over time. Like our ancestors who found fertile plains on the other side of a steep mountain, belief in your ability to impact the future actually impacts the future.

Figuring out how to put a man on the moon yielded so much more than Armstrong and Aldrin's footprints. The shock absorbers on the Oakland Bay Bridge and London's Millennium Bridge were originally designed for NASA's Apollo launchpad. The design is still used today in structures around the world. NASA created those silvery futuristic-looking space blankets that rescuers wrap around people with hypothermia to battle the bitter cold of space while being as small and light as possible. NASA invented the fireproof material used in firefighter uniforms after a cabin fire killed all three crew members on the Apollo 1 mission. NASA engineers invented that packet of vacuum-sealed deli meat in your refrigerator to ensure that astronauts would not get sick in space. The tiny camera in your cellphones and GoPros was made possible by a NASA engineer charged with making a smaller camera for space. And the compression chamber midsole used inside your running shoes was invented by a NASA Apollo engineer.

The problems solved along the way—the short-term goals—produced value independent of their long-term vision. Had NASA never made it to the moon, these discoveries would still reveal the value of their efforts.

Unlike the Boss Brain, the modern brain relishes in the comfort of zero effort. It avoids difficulty whenever possible and cuts corners to attain temporary rewards. It allows learned helplessness to validate inaction. This is not the product of 200,000 years of evolution. On the contrary, the modern brain's disdain for exertion is the product of a recent advent to society—to simply exist. To live without really trying to accomplish anything. To live effortlessly.

The modern brain tells you that the entrepreneurship game is not worth the candle and that the milk delivered directly to your door is more valuable. But being American means choosing an undertaking precisely *because* it is hard and salivating like a Pavlovian dog in anticipation of the imminent rewards that always follow tremendous effort.

The esteemed economist Israel Kirzner said that entrepreneurship is a process of discovery—where the acquisition of more and more knowledge serves as the driving force behind markets.[13] Acquisition of knowledge always requires effort. But it is not a thirst for profit or knowledge that sustains entrepreneurial efforts. The value of sustained effort lies in its ability to organize and measure the best of our skills, discover something about the world, and learn something about ourselves.

KEY POINTS

- Diligence is the difference between temporary failure and inevitable success.
- Effort is inherently costly but can also be intrinsically rewarding.
- Pretending not to want that which is challenging to obtain is just another self-deception that hides a fear of failure.
- People find more value in tasks and items that require lots of effort by them or others.
- Focusing on temporary rewards compromises the quality and duration of effort.

---

13. Israel M. Kirzner, Journal of Economic Literature Vol. 35, No. 1 (March 1997), pp. 60-85.

QUESTIONS TO ASK

- Am I willing to set my ego aside and focus on the process of developing my abilities?
- Would I prefer quick and easy short-term rewards or extended efforts that reshape my future?
- Do I feel pulled more toward actual excellence or the rewards of compliance?
- Am I focused on the process or the prize?

CHAPTER 8

THE SECOND PRIMARY INSTINCT

"THERE NEVER WAS A MOMENT, AND NEVER WILL BE,
WHEN WE ARE WITHOUT THE POWER TO ALTER
OUR DESTINY."
—STEVEN PRESSFIELD, *THE WAR OF ART*

THE SECOND PRIMARY INSTINCT: ACCOUNTABILITY

The outbreak of World War I is widely blamed on the assassination of Archduke Franz Ferdinand, the Austro-Hungarian prince whose killing led to a declaration of war on Serbia.

The Archduke's planned trip to Bosnia-Herzegovina in June of 1914 was widely publicized. Upon learning of Ferdinand's upcoming visit, a secret revolutionary society began plotting to assassinate him.

The Archduke departed for his trip even though he had received multiple death threats. A few days into his trip, Ferdinand got in an open-topped car for a motorcade ride to the Sarajevo city hall. His route had been published in advance so onlookers could line the streets and get a glimpse of him. When the motorcade passed by, a revolutionary hurled a bomb toward the Archduke's car. But the bomb bounced off the folded-up roof and rolled underneath another vehicle. The explosion wounded two army officers and several bystanders. Ferdinand was unharmed.

Rather than immediately leave the area, Ferdinand decided to continue to city hall. Upon leaving city hall, his motorcade sped away quickly to avoid any more would-be attackers. In their haste, the Archduke's chauffeur took a wrong turn and ended up on a side street right where 18-year-old revolutionary Gavrilo Princip happened to be standing. Princip pulled out his pistol and fired two shots at the Archduke from point-blank range, killing him.

It would be easy to look at the tensions that preceded WWI and blame any number of factors for the conflict. The arms race of that era, genocide, and Kaiser Wilhelm all bear some of the blame. Or perhaps one could blame the open-air motorcade, the Archduke's refusal to leave the area, or even his route being publicized in advance. While conflict was likely a foregone conclusion, the wrong turn taken by the Archduke's chauffeur sparked a domino effect that quickly led to war. His name was Leopold Lojka.

After the assassination, Lojka was forced to send three telegrams apologizing to the Austro-Hungarian Emperor, the German Emperor, and the children of Archduke Franz Ferdinand.

However, for the chauffeur to be accountable, his actions would have to meet three criteria. He would have to be in control of what transpired, he would have to develop a process to bring it about, and he would have to perceive intrinsic value in his diligence—not just the expected outcome.

For us to bear full accountability, we must take control, work within a process, and learn through diligence.

Leopold met none of those criteria. He had no way of controlling or even knowing where revolutionaries lurked. He had no plan, no process that was meant to bring about the Archduke's death. And for him, there was no value in the entire ordeal. On the contrary, it cost him his job and his reputation. He believed he was doing what needed to be done. The wrong turn didn't make him accountable. Unlike most who avoid responsibility, he genuinely was a victim of circumstance.

After our ancestors found the primary instinct of belief, they quickly encountered the burden of responsibility. They had chosen to leave the cave to test themselves on a grander stage. Along the way, accidents happened, and mistakes were made. But they could no more blame those tragedies on the first human to leave the caves than we can blame WWI on Leopold Lojka.

There will always be unforeseen challenges. Some will be minor; others might be catastrophic. Overcoming those challenges requires accountability, not blame. For us to bear full accountability, we must take control, work within a process, and learn through diligence.

THE FIRST COMPONENT OF ACCOUNTABILITY: CONTROL

Control is the first component of the Primary Instinct of Accountability. We often associate the word control with negative connotations—*that person is very controlling, I feel like I'm losing control.* However, to your Boss Brain, control means empowerment. It means that your engagement directly affects the outcome.

Our inherent fear of uncertainty is made worse by the chaos of the modern world. We are wired to choose control, but we simultaneously face the extreme expectations of the modern world that have been thrust upon us. Even higher education—which society touts as the solution to all our problems—often undermines our instincts for self-reliance. The high-powered job and elite social status that follow higher education eventually expand into a monotonous cycle of menial tasks.

Aspiring entrepreneurs face a particularly daunting challenge accepting and taking full control over the outcomes of their effort. There are no awe-filled moments, no refreshing opportunities to flex their intellectual muscle. So, the days fly by with nothing to show for them. In the end, it is easier to cede control of your life than it is to fight the system.

Fortunately, you don't have to fight the system. You can simply ignore it. Maintaining control of your life is easier when you're not worried about adhering to the system or working to raise your place within it. Only then will your self-awareness allow you to stop blaming everything around you. You'll no longer need to rewrite your past into narratives of vindication. When that happens, you are in full control.

Control is the first component of the Primary Instinct of Accountability

WAYS TO CONSCIOUSLY MAXIMIZE CONTROL

- Accept full responsibility for your current circumstances and for shaping your future. When you reject the idea that other people or things have control over your life, you permit yourself to change.

- Assess all your so-called obligations and thoughtfully consider if they can be outsourced or eliminated. Don't use them as an excuse for inaction.

- Set hard limits on the time you spend maintaining the status quo. Don't allow Parkinson's Law to expand your obligations and take over your life.

- Don't think of the past as a crystal ball to predict the future. You can rewrite your life story to explain the present, but what you do today is the only thing that will shape the future.

- Find your redemption story. Use it to garner the support of everyone and everything around you.

THE SECOND COMPONENT OF ACCOUNTABILITY: PROCESS

Process is the second component of the Primary Instinct of Accountability. We often associate processing with boring repetition. In some instances, that's true, like when we process data or forms. However, in this instance, process means your methods for getting better or the plan you intend to follow.

A process is just a way to learn and build skills. Working within a process allows you to make apples-to-apples comparisons of your results. Thus, you are empowered with the info needed to refine your efforts. Without a process to follow, you can't make comparisons and judge the results fairly. Working within a process also allows you to develop a growth mindset that isn't predicated on natural ability. In this way, processes enable you to get better and better.

Aspiring entrepreneurs can be easily overwhelmed by the enormity of the challenges that lay ahead. When they are focused on the ultimate goal and not the next step, it's hard to feel in control of the outcome. Every attempt feels like throwing darts in the dark.

Fortunately, you don't have to throw darts. You can ignore the enormity of your goal just like you can ignore society's system of control. Once you have developed a process, you only need to worry about the next step. Getting better doesn't require inspiration if you have built a system that measures your best efforts. In this way, effort becomes an art form. And all artists have a process.

Process is the second component of the Primary Instinct of Accountability

WAYS TO CONSCIOUSLY DEVELOP A MEANINGFUL PROCESS

- Tackle small steps with blinders on, and do not be discouraged by the enormity of your long-term goal.
- Find the story that is written by your relentless effort, not your natural ability. Other people will support and assist if your process redeems you in some way.
- Set a time to get to work regardless of your level of motivation. You do this every day for your job; why can't you do it for yourself?
- Utilize existing third-party systems that automate feedback on your effort so you can adjust and revise.
- Create positive reinforcements for yourself: small celebrations to acknowledge extreme effort. These are not temporary external rewards offered by others.

THE THIRD COMPONENT OF ACCOUNTABILITY: DILIGENCE

Diligence is the final component of the Primary Instinct of Account-ability. There is nothing revelatory about the importance of diligence. It's common knowledge that anything easily obtained is probably not worth having. However, there is a difference between working hard and working hard *within a process* that you control.

The true power of diligence is only realized when it is leveraged within a process. It then becomes a framework through which you gather information and discover new opportunities. For better or worse, the most valuable information is always learned by tackling the most difficult challenges. By choosing what is difficult, we learn more about ourselves and the world at the same time. Every time we fail, we learn. That is why there is intrinsic value in the pain of effort and hard work.

For aspiring entrepreneurs, the most difficult part of diligence is avoiding the temptation of chasing temporary rewards. Not only do they distract from the ultimate goal, but they also don't permanently alter behavior. Unfortunately, the most alluring temporary rewards are often the most detrimental to your diligence. They must be ignored.

Nothing is more empowering than the ability to ignore temporary rewards, to delay gratification, and to work hard while others are having fun. Working diligently within a process means proactively choosing to learn lessons today that others will learn the hard way somewhere down the road. That is the power of diligence. It arms you with knowledge and catapults you into the future.

Diligence is the third component of the Primary Instinct of Accountability

WAYS TO CONSCIOUSLY NURTURE DILIGENCE

- Systemize everything so that it can then be objectively measured and optimized.
- Acknowledge that you cannot measure your skills or test your limits without attempting difficult tasks. Choosing the easy route merely confirms the perception you have of your innate ability.
- Look for, find, and document the intrinsic value in every effort. Not only is it a good way to reference how far you've come, but it will also force you to acknowledge the lessons learned along the way.
- Recognize that temporary rewards undermine meaningful effort and treat them accordingly.

FULL ACCOUNTABILITY

Control, process, and diligence maintain the Second Primary Instinct: Accountability. Depending on the situation, you might think of accountability as either positive or negative. But that is because we often forget that lessons are learned when mistakes are made, which is always a good thing. Therefore, in the world of entrepreneurship, accountability is always positive.

Real accountability—the kind that never even considers the possibility of quitting—is often heralded as the key component of success. But when was the last time you stopped to ponder the key components of full accountability? Understanding what the word means is one thing. Understanding how to live your life that way is something else entirely. The modern world has given you the option to exhibit no accountability and still survive. The consequences are no longer fatal as they once were. As a result, it is now possible to merely float through life with no control, following no process, and displaying no diligence.

Full accountability inevitably requires that a plan be constructed, a process through which you will exert your control. The result of each plan, successful or not, teaches you something. Those lessons inspire new effort, which then requires taking control and constructing a new plan. Without the lessons learned from diligence, the cycle is broken, and accountability fades. When those lessons are embraced and used to reformulate future effort, accountability is maintained. That is how the cycle is perpetuated.

To maintain full accountability, all three components are required.

+ You can be in control without developing and working within a process.
+ You can be in control and work within a process but still lack diligence.
+ You reshape your future only when you take control and diligently work within a defined process.

BLAME IS NOT ACCOUNTABILITY

Blame and accountability are not the same thing. To be accountable is to be counted *on*. To be blamed is to be reviled or to find fault with. Accountability emphasizes reliability and performance. Blame emphasizes mistakes and discredits ability.

Blame is the opposite of accountability. It is more than just a process of assigning fault. Blaming provides a superficial and sometimes artificial solution to a complex problem. It reduces your complex reality to a simplistic view. Blame is binary; it doesn't require a process or diligence.

We live in a culture of blame. And where there is blame, there is no learning. Assigning fault makes finding solutions difficult and decreases the chances of getting to the real root of a problem. Once guilt is assigned, your modern brain stops asking questions; the process of getting better halts. The desire to understand the problem within the broader context of the whole system diminishes. Blame doesn't enhance your understanding of your situation. On the contrary, it reduces your ability to solve problems and learn from them.

Everyone makes mistakes and falls short of commitments. Being aware of your errors and viewing them as opportunities for learning and growth enables you to change the outcomes of future effort. Accountability, therefore, creates conditions for ongoing and constructive awareness of your current reality.

However, when all your energy goes into finger-pointing, scapegoating, and denying individual responsibility, productivity grinds to a halt. The problem isn't solved by determining who is at fault. The real problem is a failure to examine your current reality fearlessly. Without honest and unedited information, no one can make good decisions, and no one can advance.

Real accountability is only achieved when you take control, work within a process, and find lessons in your diligent effort, regardless of the outcome. This is the opposite of Leopold Lojka, who just accidentally took a wrong turn.

CHAPTER 9

I DON'T HAVE TIME

"ONE OF HISTORY'S FEW IRON LAWS IS THAT
LUXURIES TEND TO BECOME NECESSITIES AND TO
SPAWN NEW OBLIGATIONS."
—Yuval Harari, *Sapiens*

In 1280, a king was born in West Africa. His family ruled a kingdom that stretched for more than 2,000 miles from the Atlantic Ocean to modern-day Niger. Under his rule, the country of Mali grew exponentially. He annexed 24 cities, including what is now Timbuktu. During his reign, the Mali empire held nearly half of the world's gold. Some modern economic historians calculated the king's wealth to be half a trillion dollars, but others considered the vastness of his fortune to be indescribable. And it all belonged to King Mansa Musa, the richest man you've never heard of.

As a devout Muslim, King Musa decided to make a pilgrimage to Mecca. He organized a caravan of 60,000, including his entire royal court and officials, soldiers, local dignitaries, thousands of goats, and hundreds of camels. Each member of the convoy was clad in gold and the most exquisite Persian silk. Each camel carried hundreds of pounds of pure gold through the Saharan desert on the way to Mecca. At the time, the empire of Mali was not well known. That changed when King Musa and his golden caravan arrived in Cairo.

During his three-month stay, the king generously handed out millions of dollars worth of gold. Everyone had gold. It flowed from King Musa's caravan through the streets to everyone in northeast Africa. The natural law of supply and demand took over. Throughout the region surrounding Cairo, the value of gold plummeted for a decade. The regional economy was destroyed, causing massive turmoil throughout the Middle East for generations. Everyone blamed King Musa for the economic collapse. Those in Cairo, to whom he had so generously given gold, hated him for it.

King Musa did accomplish one thing through his excessive generosity. The Empire of Mali was no longer unknown. A map drawn in 1375 depicts Timbuktu with a drawing of an African king sitting on a golden throne holding a piece of gold in his hand. People came from near and far to see the city. Five hundred years later, Timbuktu still held mythical status as a lost city of gold. King Musa's trip to Mecca put Mali on the map. For better or for worse, his extravagant caravan and lavish lifestyle became legendary. The long trip to Mecca was his way of showing the world a glimpse of his kingdom. It was a boastful journey to self-satisfaction.

UNINTENDED CONSEQUENCES

King Musa wanted to make a name for himself, and he was willing to devote an enormous amount of resources to make that happen. Today, we create our own pilgrimage to self-satisfaction—although our caravans are to and from work. Whether you live in a large city or out in the suburbs, we now allot an enormous amount of time and resources for our commutes. And like the king's pilgrimage, there are unintended consequences to the journey.

Urban life offers expensive real estate offset by easy access to resources and jobs. Rural life provides cheap real estate with access to only natural resources and fewer jobs. It is easy to understand why most of the population has always lived in urban areas. Then, the suburbs arrived. Living in the suburbs offers cheaper real estate than urban areas and better access to resources than rural areas—a seemingly perfect balance. However, most jobs remain in urban areas. So, each morning, employees make their own pilgrimage. The average American spends twenty-six minutes each way commuting to and from their jobs—the longest commute time since the census started tracking it in 1980. And the problem is getting worse. Commutes longer than forty-five minutes are up 12%. The longest commutes, 90 minutes or more one-way, are 64% more common since 1990. Long commutes are the new normal.

One study found that people with the longest commutes are 33% more likely to suffer from depression and 21% more likely to be obese.[1] And perhaps most damaging, 46% of those with the longest commutes get less than seven hours of sleep each night.

One researcher noted, "If people are time-poor, they make poor lifestyle choices. There's a real correlation between poor nutrition, lack of exercise, and poor mental well-being." Adding 20 minutes to your daily commute has the same negative effect on job satisfaction as receiving a 19% pay cut.[2] Yet, most people still prioritize more money and their relative position within society over their free time.

Like other cultural norms, the snowballing effect of doling out small snippets of time is invisible.

Employees consistently underestimate the cumulative nature of long commutes. A recent study asked 500 people to choose between two job scenarios: Job 1 offered $64,000/year with a 20-minute commute. Job 2 offered $67,000/year with a 50-minute commute. An unbelievable 84% picked Job 2, whose longer commute is the equivalent of every waking minute of 14 days a year. Like other cultural norms, the snowballing effect of doling out small snippets of time is invisible.

Perhaps the researchers should have posed the two job scenarios differently: you can choose Job 1, which pays $64,000 with a 20-minute commute. Or you can choose Job 2, which offers $67,000 with a 20-minute commute, but there's a catch. Job 2 also requires that you

1. B. Clark, et al, "How commuting affects subjective well-being," Transportation (2019).

2. K. Chatterjee, et al, "The Commuting and Wellbeing Study: Understanding the Impact of Commuting on People's Lives," UWE Bristol, UK.

spend 14 days each year alone in your car fighting rush hour traffic for 16 hours straight. Now, which one sounds more appealing?

LOWER INPUT, SAME OUTPUT

The smartphone in your pocket has seven million times more permanent memory than the Apollo moon lander's guidance computer. That slim device that the average American stares at for nearly four hours each day has over 100,000 times the processing power of the equipment that landed on the moon 50 years ago. Such an exponential rise in computing power in the hands of the masses might lead you to believe that we are vastly more productive than Americans in the 1960s. We are not.

Just as entrepreneurship has steadily declined for the past 60 years, so too has productivity growth in the United States. Productivity grew at a tremendous rate from 1890 to 1973. Then, it inexplicably declined to pre-Civil War levels.[3] Computing power and other technological advancements saw momentous shifts in the 1970s and 1980s. However, productivity growth slowed throughout the whole U.S. economy during that period, even within sectors that invested heavily in computing power.[4] The computing capacity of the U.S. increased a hundredfold in the 1970s and 1980s, while labor productivity growth slowed from more than 3% to about 1%.[5]

This productivity paradox shows a wide discrepancy between investment in computing power and output on a global scale. Despite the ubiquity of instant information and efficiencies offered by tremendous handheld processing power, we are growing less productive.

Scientists and researchers argue about the causes of the productivity paradox. Some think that there is a lag in productivity gains. Others say that the benefits are redistributed in the economy, reducing the net increase. However, the problem with any attempt to balance an equation that requires human input is simple. Scientists assume that increasing

3. Alexander J. Field, "US Economic Growth in the Gilded Age," Journal of Macroeconomics, 31 (1): 173–190.

4. Erik Brynjolfsson, "The productivity paradox of information technology," Communications of the ACM, 36 (12): 66–77.

5. Spencer S. Jones, et al, "Unraveling the IT Productivity Paradox—Lessons for Health Care," New England Journal of Medicine, 366 (24): 2243–2245.

computing speed should increase power to produce, like a physics equation. This assumption is valid only if the other variables remain the same.

Psychology has proven that humans will do the least amount of work possible to yield adequate rewards. That's why our productivity doesn't follow the exponential curve of our computing power. Computers haven't catapulted us forward. They have empowered us to produce the same outcome with less effort.

Unlike money and effort, the usefulness of time is either wasted or redirected; it is never saved.

The contrast between expected output and input are two sides of the same coin. The entrepreneur strives for the highest possible productivity, while corporate America aims for goals based on historical precedents. Setting goals against performance that predates current tech builds procrastination and poor time management into productivity expectations. Minimum productivity levels are clearly defined, and many employees subsequently test the limits of how little work can be input to produce satisfactory results. Therefore, technological advancements don't inherently raise productivity levels. Instead, they lower the levels of required human effort.

Time is our most valuable, fragile, and perishable asset. Time expires whether we use it wisely or not, and each of us has the same number of hours and minutes available to us every day. Minutes from today cannot be spent on another day in the future. Unlike money and effort, the usefulness of time is either wasted or redirected; it is never saved.

THE COST OF TIME

Given the advent of long commutes, smartphones, and the constant distractions from the Internet, you might think that time scarcity is a recent phenomenon. But careful study will show that the modern brain's propensity to fill all our allotted time is not new.

Seneca the Younger was a stoic and philosopher who lived 2,000 years ago in the first century. In his essays entitled *On the Shortness of Life*, he shows us that while times have changed, people have not:

You are living as if destined to live forever; your own frailty
never occurs to you; you don't notice how much time has
already passed, but squander it as though you had a full
and overflowing supply—though all the while that very day
which you are devoting to somebody or something may be
your last. You act like mortals in all that you fear, and like
immortals in all that you desire.

Spending money to buy time is not a free pass to frivolously exhaust
your finances or take on debt. Financial stress induces its own set of
corrosive effects. Still, researchers have connected time scarcity to a litany
of health problems, including increased anxiety, insomnia, and obesity.
They studied whether spending money to reclaim time could positively
affect correlating adverse outcomes. The answer was a resounding yes.[6]

The published results show that working American adults reported
greater happiness and higher levels of overall life satisfaction after spending money on a time-optimizing purchase. Researchers did not see the
same effect when people used their money for material goods. The same
results emerged among the rich and poor. Everyone's well-being ben-
efited from buying time regardless of their income and financial status.

Despite the benefits of buying time, researchers found that the practice is not widespread, even among the very rich who can most definitely afford to do so. Only a slight majority of 800 millionaires recently
indicated that they spend money on time-saving tasks. The researchers
hypothesized that, at least in the United States, "we want to seem like
we have it all together, and we might be, therefore, resistant to spending
money on time-saving purchases even when we can afford it."

The American ideology values being busy above all else. This perspective creates feelings of guilt for paying someone to do an otherwise
easily accomplished task, though time-consuming. It is a peculiar aspect
of American culture that is rooted in the Protestant work ethic. Americans view hard work, discipline, and frugality as symbols of their values,

---

6. A. V. Whillans, et al, "Buying Time Promotes Happiness," *Proceedings of the National Academy of Sciences of the United States of America*, 114, no. 32: 8523-8527.

perhaps even their faith. But while America is relatively young, the problem is very old. Seneca noted:

> Aren't you ashamed to keep for yourself just the remnants
> of your life, and to devote to wisdom only that time which
> cannot be spent on any business? How late it is to begin
> really to live just when life must end! How stupid to forget
> our mortality . . .

Even 2,000 years ago, Parkinson's Law ruled our lives.

THE THREE-HOUR WORKDAY

As an experiment, the CEO of Perpetual Guardian, a New Zealand-based financial services firm, told employees who usually worked 40 hours a week to work only 32 hours, with no cut in their pay.

Logic might dictate that cutting the number of hours worked should decrease productivity. Since all the employees were salaried, the company would be paying the same amount of money for less work. Once again, the opposite occurred.

Employees at Perpetual Guardian recorded a 24% increase in work-life balance and were much more productive as a result. According to one of the researchers overseeing the study, "Supervisors said staff were more creative, their attendance was better, they were on time, and they didn't leave early or take long breaks. Their actual job performance didn't change when doing it over four days instead of five." Staff productivity remained constant while working 80% of their regular hours. It is Parkinson's Law in reverse—not because work was contracted, but because time wasn't wasted.

Corporate America almost universally operates under the presumption that you can boost productivity with salaried employees who are expected to work as many hours as possible. But that is not what happens. In reality, the average salaried employee accomplishes a little less than three hours of work each day, regardless of how many hours they physically spend at the office.[7]

7. "How Many Productive Hours in a Workday? Just 2 Hours, 23 Minutes . . ." Vouchercloud viewed at https://www.vouchercloud.com/resources/office-worker-productivity.

Long hours don't make you more productive. What matters most is your focus during the time spent working.

PUTTING YOURSELF ON THE MAP

Mother Nature designed your Boss Brain to focus on one thing at a time. Bombarding it with information reduces the quality and efficiency of your efforts. Every time you complete a small task, like posting a Tweet, sending an email, or responding to a text message, your brain gets a temporary reward in the form of dopamine. Your brain loves dopamine. That little feel-good dollop is like a free hit from a drug dealer—it keeps you coming back for more and more.

This feedback loop encourages us to rapidly complete small, manageable tasks that bring on instant gratification. But every time we redirect our focus, there's a cognitive cost. Multitasking causes a temporary but significant IQ drop similar to skipping a night of sleep or smoking marijuana.[8] It's not that we can't multitask, because technically we can. What we can't do is multi-focus.

The problem is that the chemical response during this feedback loop evolved in an era without tremendous distraction. It was Mother Nature's way to make us feel good about the smaller steps within a larger undertaking. If climbing a hill wasn't mentally rewarding, no one would climb mountains.

However, in today's world, this has become a dangerous feedback loop. The modern brain is so proud of itself each time it places a checkmark on its to-do list. Doing so makes us feel like we're accomplishing a ton when, in fact, we're just revealing our addiction to that little dopamine hit.

Multitasking also increases the production of the stress hormone cortisol. When you shift gears all day, switching from one thing to another, your brain experiences this as stress. At the end of a day filled with menial tasks, you are mentally exhausted as if those little chores were colossal.

Calculate your leisure screen time each day, then add the time you spend maintaining the life you live. Raking leaves, posting to Facebook,

---

8. C. P. Janssen, et al, "Integrating knowledge of multitasking and interruptions across different perspectives and research methods." International Journal of Human-Computer Studies, 79 pp. 1-5.

scrolling through Twitter, and fixing that squeaky door did not change anything about the state of your finances, your health, or the trajectory of your career. You feel productive, but in reality, you were just busy.

The modern brain gives away its most prized possession to put itself on the map. Drop off the dry cleaning, then post a pic to Facebook. Check your email, then look through the daily deals on Amazon. Each time you switch between tasks is like King Musa giving away gold. The more of your attention you give away, the less valuable your focus becomes.

> *The more of your attention you give away, the less valuable your focus becomes.*

Money that is lost can be earned again. Failed efforts can be tried in another way. But time that is wasted is gone forever. When the most meaningless distraction can immediately obtain your attention, the law of supply and demand takes over. What is easily obtained holds little value.

ALL THE WAY TO TIMBUKTU

King Musa was reviled in Cairo, but he returned to Mali with numerous Islamic scholars, poets, and architects. The influx of so many well-educated thinkers created a revolution of arts, culture, and architecture. The King then funded education, built schools and libraries, and commissioned the construction of the famous Djinguereber Mosque. Timbuktu became a Mecca in its own way. People traveled from around the world to study there. Private libraries sprang up inside the homes of local scholars. In a city bathed in gold, books became more valuable than any other resource.

Medieval history is filled only with stories of knights, plagues, and crusades. In that era, the European social structure was a fiefdom where one's status was determined by what he owned. But while the 'civilized' world was dividing people along economic lines, Sankoré Mosque in Timbuktu was converted into a fully staffed university boasting one of the largest libraries on the planet. Twenty-five thousand students from around the world had access to 700,000 manuscripts and scrolls.

Unlike most of us, King Musa left two legacies. One, his destructive desire for recognition and status hurt everyone but him; the other, his wise allocation of resources left an indelible mark on humanity. Here's the lesson: he was widely hated for the former and dearly loved for the latter.

WHY DOES THIS MATTER?

You likely know the balance of your bank account, but do you know the balance of each day that remains at your discretion? The dollar costs of maintaining your life are an abstraction because the benefits are temporary. The time costs, on the other hand, are concrete and permanent. Aspiring entrepreneurs must be deeply aware of the time costs created by the complexity of life, not just the dollar cost.

Focused entrepreneurship requires more than mental discipline; it requires careful manipulation of your environment, time, and resources. If you ignore the intangible costs of time wasted, you decrease the value of your focused attention. As discussed in Chapter 2, the system is designed to process, not to produce. When you give in to the urge to fill your day with low-value tasks, you become the middleman between those who pay you and those you must pay. It's money in, money out. You trade dollars for a to-do list.

If you accepted Job 2 because you think the extra $3,000 is worth it, know this: a salary of $67,000/year is about $32/hour. Choosing that scenario only pays you $11.50 for the additional hour commuting each day. That's roughly a third of your regular compensation before subtracting for gas and other costs.

The modern brain is so addicted to self-satisfaction and the feeling of accomplishment that we jump from task to task all day, even though many of those tasks have no long-term significance. We value items more when they require more time to build or obtain, but we rarely calculate the time it takes to earn the price of our purchases. And those purchases spawn more obligations that require more time. We obligate ourselves and blame our obligations, just as we surround ourselves with distractions and then blame them for distracting us.

Time isn't money. The phrase was popularized by the belief that we are paid for our time, not our productivity. But that is not the case. In traditional employment, you agree to the value of your time before working, but you are not paid until after the work is completed. The work carries no value to you if you are not paid. Therefore, your employer buys your productivity, but you sell your future.

KEY POINTS

- Your environment is the single biggest threat to where and how you apply your attention.
- Flaunting status is the quickest way to lose it.
- The same spirit that inspires Americans to dream of self-employment also causes us to waste time on menial tasks.
- Tech advances undermine effort and productivity. Time cannot be saved.
- There is a physical and mental difference between being busy and being productive.

QUESTIONS TO ASK

- How can I outsource menial tasks that do not add value to my legacy? Do I use menial tasks as an excuse for inaction?
- Does my screen time add tangible value to life or contribute to my long-term plan?
- Do I make use of the time afforded to me by tech advancements, or do I simply reduce my effort proportionally?
- Am I proactive or reactive? Do I plan my days or deal with them as they come?
- Do I know the balance of each day that remains at my discretion?

CHAPTER 10

ONE DAY I WILL

"A MAN WHO PROCRASTINATES IN HIS CHOOSING
WILL INEVITABLY HAVE HIS CHOICE MADE FOR HIM BY
CIRCUMSTANCE."
—HUNTER S. THOMPSON, *THE PROUD HIGHWAY*

The catastrophic events of WWI inspired many engineers and artists to rethink what the future would look like. They began to reject traditional education where each subject was separated and taught in a bubble. Instead, they blended science and art into one school of thought. One group of architects, artists, and engineers forged a new philosophy that shaped the modern world. They merged science and creativity. Not creativity as an individual expression, but the type that emerges by removing everything unnecessary.

Their ideology became an actual school when Bauhaus, a school of design, architecture, and applied arts, was founded in Germany in 1919. Bauhaus didn't target specific professions. At its core, the school intended to eliminate all the unnecessary parts of any creation regardless of the subject. The Bauhaus philosophy prevented designers from expressing their unique style during the creation process. Instead, students were trained equally in art and technical craftsmanship. The goal was to end the long-standing divide that had always existed between the two.

This may sound utterly unrelated to entrepreneurship, except for the fact that the Bauhaus philosophy played a significant role in designing many of the items you own today and in creating one of the world's most valuable companies.

When Jony Ive joined Apple at the age of 26, he was already steeped in the Bauhaus tradition. The tradition wasn't a blind commitment to minimalism. It was a design approach that considers all aspects like necessity, function, cost, and rationality. Aesthetic was not primary. Instead, purpose rendered aesthetic. When asked about his simple, minimalist designs, Ive answered:

> With physical products, we have to feel we can dominate them. As you bring order to complexity, you find a way to make the product defer to you. Simplicity isn't just a visual style. It's not just minimalism or the absence of clutter. It involves digging through the depth of the complexity. To be truly simple, you have to go really deep . . . in order to be able to get rid of the parts that are not essential.

Ive's commitment to Bauhaus ideology produced the iMac, iPod, iPad, MacBook, MacBook Air, and the iPhone. The success of these products cascaded through the industry and the world. Today, complexity in the retail marketplace is shunned and mocked. Products that lack an obvious purpose rarely succeed.

The lesson, like the Bauhaus philosophy, is simple: form follows function. When you bring order to the complexity of your world, it defers to you. When the individual components of your

When the individual components of your world are distilled and concentrated into only that which has a purpose, you can dominate everything around you.

world are distilled and concentrated into only that which has a purpose, you can dominate everything around you.

DOMINATE OR BE DOMINATED

Staples of the modern world are often easily replaced, even disposable. The usefulness of the items that add value to our lives is quickly exhausted or made obsolete by newer designs. Each week, we stack a procession of single-use luxuries in our recycle bins and place them by the curb to be removed from our lives. We dominated them. They served their purpose and are now of no more use to us.

However, a problem occurs when luxuries become necessities. When circumstances prevent access to them, even temporarily, we have no idea what to do with our time or how to function in their absence. Do you remember the last time a storm knocked out power to your home? How did you spend the time with no TV and no Internet? The frustration each of us experiences when we don't have a strong cell signal perfectly exemplifies our total reliance on items that were once considered luxuries.

Society has become so dependent on disposable items that we spend valuable time obtaining what we intend to discard. Every day, new services emerge that allow us to dominate how our time is used, but very few of us utilize them. A study in 2019 found that 81% of Americans own a smartphone, and nearly 80% own a computer with access to the Internet. Although, each year, almost 45%, or 6.45 billion bill payments are still paid by mailing a check. A long list of retail stores and grocers offer online ordering with delivery or curbside pickup. Nevertheless, before the COVID-19 virus outbreak of 2020, 81% of consumers had never ordered groceries online.

We dominate single-use items and toss them aside, yet we allow the procurement and maintenance of those items to burn massive amounts of our time. The net gain of time saved through their usage is likely less than the time spent in their acquisition. So, who is dominating whom?

The average cost of monthly yard maintenance in America is less than the average spent monthly on cable TV. For would-be entrepreneurs, this yields a massive swing in the wrong direction. Homeowners end up spending an average of 1,460 hours per year watching TV and 70 hours a year mowing grass. Those two comprise the equivalent of every waking hour of 96 days a year.

If the average homeowner canceled cable and used the money to hire a maintenance service, more than three months of free time would be recaptured each year. Again, every waking minute of more than three months.

What if you already cut the cord? Well, the average U.S. household also spends an estimated $850 annually on soft drinks. Therefore, a family could eliminate soft drinks from their diet, gain tremendous health benefits, and still have enough cash to pay for lawn maintenance.

The most profound takeaway from the Bauhaus movement wasn't the value of simplicity or reductionism—it was reasoning. Bauhaus philosophy encourages designers to give up all the unnecessary things added out of custom. They are taught to discard the details that serve only to make something more aesthetically pleasing. Their goal is to understand the reason why every single component of a design is necessary. And make no mistake, each of us designs our own life.

PROCRASTINATION AND THE DEADLINE

Enough has been said about the ubiquity of procrastination. But until 2007, its causes were mostly presumptions. That year, a psychologist named Piers Steel wrote a paper that finally showed the origins of procrastination. Fortunately, Piers Steel has the name of a film noir private investigator because his research required some serious detective work to finally catch the thief of time.

Steel used meta-analysis, which allowed him to combine all the data from decades of research on procrastination. The results proved that the two oldest theories for why we procrastinate—anxiety and rebelliousness—show only a weak correlation.

On the other hand, four factors emerged as the strongest true predictors of procrastination. They were low self-efficacy, low value, impulsiveness, and delay.[1]

As discussed in Part 1, low self-efficacy is a lack of belief that we can complete a task. The likelihood of procrastination skyrockets when we

---

1. Piers Steel, "The nature of procrastination: a meta-analytic and theoretical review of quintessential self-regulatory failure," Psychol Bull 133: 65-94. 10.1037/0033-2909.133.1.65.

don't have confidence in our ability to do something. This happens most often when we're uncertain about how even to begin a task.

As discussed in Part 2, the more value we find in a task, the more likely we will enjoy it and the less we procrastinate before starting it.

As discussed in the preceding chapter, impulsiveness is due largely to a lack of focus in the face of immediate and more appealing distractions. When immersed in a highly distracting environment, we're much more likely to procrastinate.

And finally, there is delay. Delay is the time between the decision to take on a task and its deadline. The longer you have to finish a task, the longer you'll wait to get started on it.

The term *deadline* originated in prison camps during the American Civil War. More specifically, Andersonville Prison outside Americus, Georgia. At Andersonville, a fence known as 'the dead line' was erected inside the prison walls. Anyone crossing or even touching the dead line was shot without warning.

The conditions at Andersonville were inhumane. Those who didn't starve usually died of dysentery, typhoid fever, or murder. The Georgia summers were brutal, and there was no wood for fires in the winter. The only source of drinking water was a creek that also served as the latrine. Prisoners who reached their mental or physical limits would sometimes purposefully walk past the dead line to end their suffering.

Without setting a deadline for a task, it's easy to feel as if you have limitless time to complete it. Therefore, you delay starting. The Stoic philosopher Seneca said:

> Putting things off is the biggest waste of life: it snatches away each day as it comes and denies us the present by promising the future. The greatest obstacle to living is expectancy.

Seneca spoke timeless truth—it's difficult to start something with no expectancy and no immediate benefit. That's because the rewards arrive when something is accomplished, not when it is first started.

The last day of your life is not your last opportunity to start something. It's your last chance to finish. If you treat the deadline of your life

as the deadline to start a project, then the present will always be filled
with dread and the future with regret.

POVERTY OF TIME

In 1985, the Sri Lankan government forced nearly 300 villagers to give
up their homes and resettle in a different location. Each villager received
2.5 hectares and a government grant to offset the burden of resettlement.
Ten years later, thirty were successful entrepreneurs. The rest were living
in a state of necessity, what would typically be called hand-to-mouth or
paycheck-to-paycheck. Many of them worked for the thirty entrepreneurs. The study showed how the two groups ended up in such different
circumstances, despite starting with the same assets.[2]

With their newfound windfall, the hand-to-mouth villagers spent
lavishly on social enhancements and signs of status. They did not save.
They soon acquired debt and became trapped in a cycle of constant need.
Lack of resources forced them to lease most of their land to the entrepreneurs. Most of them survived by selling their labor to their more prosper-
ous neighbors and were forced to commute long distances to do their
work. Even when harvests were excellent, and they earned more, any
surplus went toward paying off debt. They squandered their resources.

When asked why they didn't start a more profitable venture, they
replied that they had no surplus capital and were simply too tired to do
anything else at the end of the day. They were effectively trapped in a
cycle of debt and need. Their income took all their energy and time, yet
it was barely enough to pay their debts and survive. They could spare no
time or money for entrepreneurship.

Even when asked what business they would start if resources and time
made themselves available, none had any idea what they would do. They
were so used to being trapped that they had ceased to consider alternatives.

In contrast, the successful villagers saved their cash, avoided debt,
and expanded their businesses. They sacrificed symbols of social status
in the short term and invested their money in ways that didn't yield
temporary rewards. One entrepreneur bought a tractor instead of a nicer
house. He built a brick garage to protect his tractor even while living in a

---

2. Peter Rosa, et al, "Entrepreneurial Motivation in Developing Countries: What does "Necessity" and
"Opportunity" Entrepreneurship Really Means?" Frontiers of Entrepreneurship Research , 26, 531-544.

grass hut. Ironically, the most dilapidated housing in the villages usually belonged to the most successful entrepreneurs.

> *There is no poverty like poverty of time.*

There is no poverty like poverty of time. Just like a middle-class suburbanite with a two-hour commute each day, the villagers were in constant need of more time. They showed no signs of entrepreneurial effort because entrepreneurship is not born of necessity—quite the opposite. Necessity is, in fact, one of the main barriers to entrepreneurship.

TINY HOUSES AND BIG CLOSETS

Christopher Walken's famous cameo as Captain Koons in the movie *Pulp Fiction* is the perfect example of the power that attachments, particularly those with a meaningful backstory, have over our lives. In the scene, Walken is given an heirloom watch by a dying soldier in a Vietnamese prison camp. Walken must deliver it to the dead man's son. The watch itself wasn't valuable, but it became the single trigger for a hilarious yet deadly calamity of events because of its history. From great-grandfather to grandfather to father, the watch bounced through history from one war to the next until given to a young Bruce Willis after an epic monologue from Walken explaining its significance. In the movie, Willis nearly dies trying to recover the lost watch.

Our sense of self includes the things we can control and the things we own. Even when objects no longer serve a useful purpose, our connection to them runs deep if they are part of our personal story. *That unused teapot was a wedding gift from my dead aunt. The broken rocking chair in the garage belonged to my great-grandmother.* Everything carries the weight of memory. These items help us construct identities that transcend time. Parting with them feels like parting with a piece of ourselves.

However, heirlooms and mementos do not necessarily occupy our time or cause us to procrastinate. All the other meaningless bulk that fills our lives does that for us. Simplifying and decluttering has become a new obsession for millions of people. Yet despite popular shows touting minimalism, downsizing, and tiny houses, Americans now own more stuff than any time in history. Valuing experiences above objects is a popular message on social media, but consumerism is still at an all-time high.

Finding room for the material overflow of the new American dream has proven tough. About 10% of Americans now pay an average of $91.14 per month for self-storage. According to a company that tracks the self-storage industry, America has more than 50,000 self-storage facilities, which offer 2.3 billion square feet of rentable space. The volume of self-storage units could fill the Hoover Dam more than 26 times.

We sacrifice what can never be replaced to obtain items that are rarely used and then willfully discarded.

We rarely consider the mental weight of material possessions, nor do we measure the resources they consume against their value. Materialism makes us feel powerful while simultaneously taking power away. With each item purchased, you are giving up time and money. The upside is that buying new stuff provides a temporary boost, but that quickly fades and reveals an even greater downside. The cost of every item stacked in your closet or storage unit is permanent. The benefit they provide is not.

We choose poverty of time over poverty of wealth, which is the true irony of materialism and social status. We sacrifice what can never be replaced to obtain items that are rarely used and then willfully discarded.

WHY DOES THIS MATTER?

To maintain focus, would-be entrepreneurs must be the architects of their environment first. You can dominate a well-designed environment.

In the Bauhaus tradition, you must level the distinction between art and engineering by reuniting your inherent creativity with your productivity. The more resistant you are to tradition, the more your outcomes will differ from the rest of society. But controlled attention is much more difficult to maintain than stimulus-driven attention. Therefore, the problem exists at a micro and macro level. While Facebook serves as a pleasant distraction at the micro-level, many would-be entrepreneurs waste weeks out of their year on larger distractions on the macro level. Being busy makes us feel productive at the expense of true productivity.

There is a difference between time management and productivity. The American ideal of always being busy hasn't translated into higher productivity. In fact, we have become individually less productive as the nation's productivity has increased. Just as entrepreneurship decreases as quality of life metrics increase, so too does productivity. All the technological advancements of the computer age decreased the effort required to produce the same results.

As the complexity of life increases, the value of yielded outcomes decreases. We are now in maintenance mode, processing not producing. The aspiring entrepreneur, especially one who has spent their whole life as an employee, must recognize the permanent costs of possessions in both time and money and weigh them against the temporary benefits they provide. You could outsource or automate the trivial, eliminating the tools and time needed to maintain the status quo. But history shows that doing so doesn't yield higher productivity. Instead, we end up reducing our effort and procrastinate by occupying our time in wasteful ways.

Maintaining your current lifestyle stabilizes the future but does not reshape it. The only sustainable way to increase productivity and change the future is to redirect more time and effort toward different outcomes and less toward maintaining existing conditions. Maintenance, by definition, ensures that tomorrow looks just like yesterday.

The modern brain uses materialism to offset the pain of a compromised existence. Sure, materialism can provide a kind of joy—the temporary thrill of purchasing something new and the ego-inflating opportunities to show it off. But with possessions come obligations. And no matter how many items you purchase, you cannot buy your way out of a compromised existence.

KEY POINTS

- ◆ All your resources should be directed toward your ultimate goal, not toward temporary rewards.
- ◆ Simplicity enhances utility.

- Outsourcing time-consuming tasks leads to higher levels of productivity and greater focus.
- Squandering wealth will result in poverty of both time and money.
- The benefits of materialism are temporary. The costs are permanent.
- Possessions spawn obligations. What you own ends up owning you.

QUESTIONS TO ASK

- Do the things I own provide more than fleeting pleasure or temporary benefit?
- Would I trade the things I own for a thriving business?
- If I had to leave home forever, what do I own that is worth carrying with me?
- Is most of my time spent on maintenance of my existing conditions or growth toward my goals?

CHAPTER 11

I DON'T HAVE THE MONEY

"WORRYING IS LIKE PAYING A DEBT YOU DON'T OWE."
—MARK TWAIN

The Italian poet Dante Alighieri completed his epic narrative *The Divine Comedy* in 1320. The poem describes the nine levels of Hell, each more horrific than the last. As a person's wickedness grows more and more sinister, he is condemned to an ever-deeper level of Hell. While the upper levels are designed for amateur offenders, like virtuous pagans and the unbaptized, the lower levels are for the truly wicked. Level seven is reserved as the site of eternal damnation for murderers, rapists, and . . . greedy money lenders.

Man's love-hate relationship with lending money dates back thousands of years. Some of the earliest lending laws were written, not surprisingly, in the same region of the world where the word *entrepreneur* originated. The ancient Hindu Code of Manu established clear instructions on how to lend money and the terms that fall within moral standards.

Various countries and religions set their own ethical standards for lending throughout the centuries, and today's loan and mortgage laws are some of the most complex. Coincidentally, the rise of the American mortgage began its ascent at the same place in history where entrepreneurship started its descent. The mortgage-backed housing market in the

U.S. started growing in 1949 and continued through the housing crisis in 2008. Nearly six decades of housing growth.

The American government caused this rapid growth by establishing a new system that decreased lenders' liability. This system increased the national mortgage debt-to-income ratio in America from 20% to 73%. During the same period, the ratio of mortgage debt to household assets also rose from 15% to 41%.

As the definition of the American Dream shifted away from self-employment and toward homeownership, the 30-year mortgage became the most popular way to buy a home. The very same Americans who could not find the will to invest in themselves lined up to acquire enormous amounts of debt via a home mortgage.

The average person spends 110 minutes a day on household activities. That is the equivalent of every waking minute of 42 days a year.[1] The average homeowner also spends $1200 per year on home maintenance, $1,100 per year on home insurance, $2,300 per year in property taxes, and $500 per year on furnishings. That's $5,100 each year that just disappears.

The median mortgage payment in America is around $1100 per month, and the median household bring-home income is $44,000. That means the average family spends 42 cents of every bring-home dollar toward homeownership. That's every dime the average American household earns in five months. And this is before electric bills, car payments, phone bills, grocery bills, school supplies, gas, and car insurance.

For the average American whose income is capped by the limits of their job, homeownership isn't a dream, it's economic entrapment. And homeownership isn't the only form of debt sucking away resources.

SUPERSIZED SPENDING

In 1992, McDonald's began offering customers the chance to supersize their French fries and soft drinks. Previously, they only offered the traditional small, medium, or large. Their customers had not changed. Caloric demand was no higher. Patrons weren't hungrier than before. Still, the option was a hit, and customers supersized their combos. That marketing plan revealed a strange and never before documented phenomenon.

---

1. "American Time Use Survey," Bureau of Labor Statistics viewed at https://www.bls.gov/tus/charts/household.htm.

In the 30 years that followed, the size of retail food packaging and restaurant portions steadily increased. In 2005, obesity researchers proved that increases in package and portion size increased consumption, even when the caloric density of the food was higher.

When food is abundant, we simply consume more.

Scientists eventually concluded that bigger portions and packaging suggest higher consumption norms. In other words, the amount of food on a plate or in a bowl implies what might be considered a reasonable amount to eat. Larger portions prime our brains to eat more. Package and portion size influence how much people expect to consume, and thereby change how much they actually consume.[2]

In 2020, the total credit card debt in America hit an all-time high of $930 billion. The laws of frugality might lead some people to expect high levels of credit card debt when the economy isn't doing as well. The opposite is true.

Before the COVID-19 outbreak in early 2020, the economy was roaring. The unemployment rate was at a 50-year low, and wages were rising. Historically, household debt is highest when the unemployment rate is low. Families find themselves comfortable enough to invite risk. But instead of risking a new business startup, they traditionally take on more personal debt.

Nearly 40 million Americans earn less than $15 per hour. A 2018 Federal Reserve survey found that only 61% of Americans could cover an unexpected expense of $400 without borrowing money. According to Experian, Americans held an average of $6,500 in credit card debt at the end of 2019.

When the economy is soaring and borrowers are flush with cash, hungry lenders are motivated to extend more. Credit card limits increase, and families take on more credit card debt. Instead of saving some of their fries for when times are lean, they eat them all now. Borrowing needs haven't changed, but higher credit limits imply that higher spending is normal. Larger available balances prime our brains to purchase more. Credit limits influence how much money people expect to spend, and thereby change how much they actually spend.

---

2. Brian Wansink, et al, "Bottomless bowls: why visual cues of portion size may influence intake," Obes Res. 2005;13:93–100.

When credit is abundant, we simply spend more.

However, when debt levels exceed income levels, the process is reversed. Cardholders struggle to service debt at the exact moment when jobs and cash are scarce, making lenders more hesitant to extend credit. Historically speaking, credit is least available when would-be entrepreneurs are most in need of it.

One might argue that the problem is low wages, and people are subsequently forced to use credit to pay for essentials. But that is not how most Americans use debt.

DOUGH AND DOUGHNUTS

Imagine you walk into the company break room and find a dozen doughnuts. They are the classic kind that is round with a hole in the middle, not jam-filled or crullers or eclairs. Think of that doughnut before the hole was cut. The part of the dough that got removed to create the hole isn't the hole. The hole is what remains after that part was removed. So, is the hole a thing? Was it there all along and only revealed by removing the center part of the dough? Or, are holes not even a thing, just the absence of a thing? It is a philosophical question: are holes actually things themselves or, as the writer Kurt Tucholsky suggested in *The Social Psychology of Holes*, are they just "where something isn't"?

Those who carry credit card debt outspend debt-free households in seven of nine discretionary spending categories.

If you dig a hole and carefully maintain what is removed, you can use it to re-fill the hole. However, if you spread the dirt around, the only way to fill the first hole is to dig another hole.

Debt is a hole. Once dug, the only way to fill it without digging another hole is to manage the yielded cash carefully. But that is not how most Americans use debt. Instead, we spread that dirt around.

A 2019 CreditCards.com poll showed that those who carry credit card debt outspend debt-free households in seven of nine discretionary spending categories. The average American family spends thousands of dollars a year on discretionary purchases using credit cards. With the average credit card interest rate at 18%, they're paying a steep price for the privilege of instant gratification. And what's worse, they're spreading that debt around by purchasing travel, clothes, and expensive meals.

Most credit cards require you to pay only 1% or 2% of the balance each month plus fees and interest. But making these small payments won't make any real progress on paying down your balance. If an average cardholder manages to pay $100 each month toward the average credit card balance, it will take more than 20 years to fill that hole and will cost more than $18,000 in interest. Would you be willing to pay $24,500 for all the products and experiences that the original $6500 in debt provided?

Debt is not necessarily a bad thing, so long as the proceeds are managed properly. However, when the proceeds are spread around, the only way to fill that hole is to dig another hole. If debt is a hole, then it is most definitely a real thing, not just where something isn't. And in the words of the famous cowboy Will Rogers, "When you find yourself in a hole, stop digging."

LACK OF MONEY OR LACK OF DISCIPLINE

Small businesses are the lifeblood of the U.S. economy. America's 30 million small businesses play a critical role in job creation and retention. In the last 20 years, small businesses have created more than 65% of all new jobs. They also drive our productivity through innovation and competitiveness. In fact, small companies transact 44% of the U.S. economic activity. The engine of small business in the U.S. is powered largely by the United States Small Business Administration (SBA).

The SBA is the world's largest business loan guarantor. It offers loan guarantees for small businesses that may not qualify for traditional bank loans. After the great recession, the SBA's top priority was to make lending more accessible to small business owners. By early 2020, the SBA lending programs were performing at record levels.

In 2019 alone, the SBA guaranteed more than 70,000 loans totaling $28.9 billion, an all-time high in SBA lending. Remarkably, it happened without any subsidy from the American taxpayer. Minority business owners received $8.8 billion, and women-owned businesses received nearly $8.1 billion.

Beyond the SBA, there are private equity firms, private lenders, venture capitalists, and, of course, traditional loans. To put it bluntly, America has greater access to entrepreneurial capital than any country on the planet. Simultaneously, self-employment in the U.S. ranks among the lowest in the world. As America's prosperity increases, so do the opportunities to leverage our cash in ways that bring immediate gratification. Money is not the problem; the problem is how we use it.

SENDING GOOD MONEY AFTER BAD

English is a melting pot of words and phrases adopted from other languages. Aside from its propensity to set and systematically break arbitrary grammar rules, learning English is further complicated by the incessant use of idiomatic phrases with hidden meanings. These colloquialisms are often made more confounding by the sensitivity of the topic to which they pertain. In the American south, any subject that is too taboo to speak about publicly in plain English is usually discussed via a host of euphemisms and metaphors.

Sex and stupidity are delicate subjects in the Bible Belt. So instead of using the terms outright, southerners employ a hilarious and sometimes brutal list of alternative expressions to soften the blow while impugning someone's virtue or intelligence. Given America's emotional and complicated relationship with money, it is not surprising that we handle financial discussions with similar delicacy.

English has dozens of ways to imply that a purchase or endeavor is a complete waste of money. However, none quite fit the bill for Congress' recent two billion dollar "investment" of tax-payer dollars in Amtrak.

Over the past 20 years, St. Louis Lambert International Airport has seen a major decline in service. After losing their hub status with American Airlines, much of Concourse D was shut down during 2008 when Lambert saw nearly seven million fewer travelers. In 2009, American Airlines cut flights to Lambert from around 200 daily to 36. Even with Southwest Airlines adding flights there, cost-saving measures at one point forced the closure of 36 of the airport's 86 total gates.

At the end of a 20-year struggle to rebuild St. Louis as a travel destination, Amtrak received and spent two billion dollars of taxpayer money to increase the speed of their trains from Chicago to St. Louis. The goal was to cut the five-and-a-half-hour trip down to four-and-a-half hours. But that did not happen. Instead, the project could only achieve speeds that netted about a 15-minute reduction in travel time. However, even that gain didn't guarantee passengers would benefit.

The Amtrak trip between Chicago and St. Louis is not even within the top 15 of their most on-time trips. More than a third of the time, the train is late. The increased speeds are then nullified. This "fast-rail project" is anything but fast. Meanwhile, American Airlines, who previously cut hundreds of flights to St. Louis, still flies there from Chicago seven times per day . . . in about an hour.

Call it money down the drain or sending good money after bad, but taxpayers cannot afford to point the dirty end of the stick. The average American home has a dishwasher, a washer and dryer, hot water, an oven, an electric range, and a refrigerator. Each of these appliances functions automatically and makes otherwise difficult tasks simple. One hundred years ago, they would have been considered luxuries. Now, they blend into the background of our lives.

> *Black Friday grows bigger and bigger as our individual productivity falls lower and lower.*

But what has that investment netted us? Labor productivity rates have trended downward since these inventions became commonplace. In the late 1940s, our non-farm labor productivity growth rates averaged 3.6%. As of 2016, that number had fallen to 1.1%. Our individual productivity grows at less than a third of the rate that our grandparents achieved.[3]

The money we invest in getting us to our destination quicker is wasted if we depart too late to arrive on time. Each year, new gadgets and faster appliances hit the market to "save" us more and more time. Your dishwasher cleans your coffee mug while you watch TV, and your

3. Shawn Sprague, "Below trend: the U.S. productivity slowdown since the Great Recession," *Beyond the Numbers: Productivity*, vol. 6, no. 2 (U.S. Bureau of Labor Statistics, January 2017),

automatic coffee maker lets you sleep a few minutes longer each morning. Black Friday grows bigger and bigger as our individual productivity
falls lower and lower. Simultaneously, a study by the Center for Disease
Control and Prevention determined in 2019 that Americans average
more than five hours of discretionary time each day.[4]

There is nothing wrong with buying or using modern conveniences.
Just be sure that as you upgrade your appliances, you don't downgrade
the expectations you have of yourself.

THE COURAGE OF HONESTY

Brené Brown is a research professor at the University of Houston who
is best known for her famous TED Talk, *The Power of Vulnerability*. She
has molded that message into multiple best-selling books and a tsunami
of loyal followers. Her message swelled in popularity, at least in part,
because Americans needed to feel comfortable being vulnerable:

> Vulnerability is not winning or losing; it's having the
> courage to show up and be seen when we have no control
> over the outcome. Vulnerability is not weakness; it's our
> greatest measure of courage . . . People who wade into
> discomfort and vulnerability and tell the truth about their
> stories are the real badasses.

Brown has spent nearly two decades studying courage, vulnerability,
shame, and empathy. And her message was one that aspiring entrepreneurs needed to hear. For the first time, an authority on human behavior
stood on stage and was brave enough to say that it is okay to admit that
you don't have everything together. Brown's talk not only permitted us
to display our vulnerability but also pointed out the incredible courage
required to do so.

Historically, would-be entrepreneurs would stand among their possessions or enjoy lavish lifestyles while simultaneously decrying lack of
capital as the reason for their entrepreneurial inaction. Before Brown's

---

4. R. Sturm and D. A. Cohen, "Free Time and Physical Activity Among Americans 15 Years or Older:
Cross-Sectional Analysis of the American Time Use Survey," Prev Chronic Dis 2019;16:190017.

message, to admit their mistakes and subsequent vulnerability implied weakness. Instead, they would put on a brave face and pretend to have everything together.

But Brown's message of empowerment brought pride to self-awareness. It made transparency tolerable. Vulnerability, according to Brown, is our most accurate measurement of courage. Taking ownership of your financial circumstances and admitting irresponsibility doesn't make you a buffoon; it makes you a badass.

To the immature entrepreneur who has spent his life squandering resources, the pain of pretending was less than the humiliation of honesty. But as his secrets grew, so too did his shame. To the Boss Brain, however, the pride of humility vastly outweighs any pretense of self-image.

Today, we can finally admit to ourselves and others that blaming everything but ourselves isn't brave. It's cowardly.

WHY DOES THIS MATTER?

Small businesses generate nearly half of the country's economic output. Startup resources are everywhere. The SBA even offers free training for those who feel they need help. Nowhere in the world provides a more supportive environment for the entrepreneurial spirit than America.

The problem isn't a lack of available capital. The problem is that most of our wealth is squandered on non-essentials. The painful truth is that most would-be entrepreneurs either lack the courage to accept responsibility for their financial circumstances, or they lack the discipline to make changes to their spending habits.

Your blessings, like all gifts, come at a cost. The price you pay isn't always immediate, but it is permanent. Each person has a unique tolerance for the pain of delayed gratification. And change only comes when being broke becomes more painful than sacrificing social status, luxury experiences, and material possessions.

Would-be entrepreneurs jump at the chance to acquire a lifetime of financial obligation while shunning the idea of investing a fraction of that amount in themselves. They ignore the ultimate costs to their peril. Once they have dug themselves into a hole, they usually decide just to keep digging.

The modern brain exchanges irreplaceable resources for temporary benefits. Owning a home is not a bad thing unless you need the flexibility to relocate to thriving markets or the agility to reallocate resources in times of scarcity. Massive financial obligations create a poverty of time, in addition to the poverty of money. The two form a debt cycle. Making minimum payments means maintaining current conditions. At that point, you are stuck.

The Boss Brain, however, has no use for non-essentials. They only detract from the goal. It finds no joy in fleeting pleasures that hold no long-term value. On the contrary, it revels in the pain of self-sacrifice, knowing that temperance and restraint will yield dividends long after paying their price.

KEY POINTS

- Massive financial obligations create a poverty of time. Unlike money, time can never be saved.
- Massive debt hinders an entrepreneur's agility and ability to respond to ever-changing markets.
- Poverty of wealth will inevitably result in poverty of time.
- Credit availability primes our brain to spend more.
- There are virtually limitless funding resources available to aspiring American entrepreneurs.
- Money spent on tech and other modern luxuries rarely yields a measurable return.
- Having honesty and transparency regarding financial matters takes incredible courage.

QUESTIONS TO ASK

- Do I have a budget that includes saving startup capital for my future business?
- What would I lose by selling everything I own? What would I gain?
- Can I find meaning in sacrifice, knowing that it brings me closer to my goals?
- Do I really lack capital, or do I just need more discipline?

CHAPTER 12

THE THIRD PRIMARY INSTINCT

"WORK AS HARD AS YOU POSSIBLY CAN ON ONE THING
AND SEE WHAT HAPPENS."
—JORDAN PETERSON

THE THIRD PRIMARY INSTINCT: FOCUS

Napoleon defeated the Prussian Army at Ligny in June of 1815. Afterward, he reallocated a third of his resources and sent 33,000 men to pursue the retreating Prussians. A few days later, Napoleon led his remaining 72,000 troops against the Duke of Wellington's 68,000-man army at Waterloo.

It had heavily rained the night before, and the battlefield was muddy. The environment was too wet, in Napoleon's opinion. He decided to wait until the ground dried before ordering his men to attack.

What he didn't know was the remains of the defeated Prussian Army had eluded his men and were on the march to Waterloo to join The Duke of Wellington. Napoleon was so distracted by the muddy ground that he waited until midday to attack. The time he wasted allowed the Prussians to join the battle. They attacked Napoleon's right flank in the late afternoon, and the French Army was soundly defeated.

Napoleon made poor use of his resources when he divided his army. His wet environment was an enormous distraction that ultimately cost him time. And the time he wasted carried no value without victory. Napoleon was not focused in this battle, and that cost him the war.

To be a focused entrepreneur, you must not allow your environment to affect your productivity. You must thoughtfully allocate your resources, and you must spend time in ways that carry intrinsic value.

THE FIRST COMPONENT OF FOCUS: ENVIRONMENT

Environment is the first component of the Primary Instinct of Focus. The word environment is usually used to describe some intangible quality of where you live or work. However, to your Boss Brain, your environment is more than just places and times in which you might temporarily find yourself. Instead, it is the backdrop that directs the story of your life.

Before any Broadway show begins, the stage is set. The environment helps us better understand and anticipate the part that each character plays. From there, we take cues on how to feel, how to think, and how to react. As spectators, the journey we take has no unintended consequences. That's why we enjoy theater—it allows us to live in an imaginary world temporarily. But the characters on stage are bound by it. They can't escape the fiction built on the stage around them . . . and we can't escape the fiction built around us in the real world either.

Every aspiring entrepreneur is on stage in one way or another, and the backdrop that directs your life story changes how you feel, think, and act. As your environment improves, life gets easier, and the expectations you have of yourself decrease along with your productivity. That's why you must purposefully avoid building an environment that is too comfortable. Comfort creates complacency and reduces your productivity. A stark, minimalist environment reduces the chaos on your stage and empowers you to better understand and anticipate what will happen next. Otherwise, you'll end up spending most of your time reacting, not acting. Until you purposefully and consciously manufacture your environment, you are doomed to become a product of it.

At this point, you already have the belief and accountability needed to manufacture an environment that is conducive to entrepreneurship. Look around . . . nearly everything you see is the backdrop for a play that you no longer star in. Instead, build your own stage. After you do that, you can play any part you want.

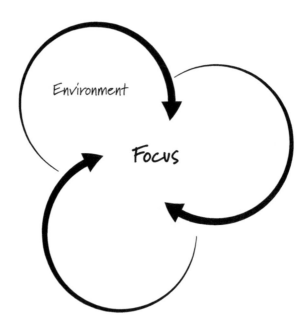

Environment is the first component of the Primary Instinct of Focus

WAYS TO ENGINEER YOUR ENVIRONMENT

- Find pleasure in sacrifice and avoid temporary rewards. In today's world, delaying gratification is a rare ability. Like everything else, the rarer it becomes, the more valuable it will be.
- Recognize the cascading effect of small and large purchases that could immobilize you mentally and physically. The unintended consequences of possessions are often hidden in plain sight.
- Find and utilize every available tool to automate your life. And don't subsequently lower your efforts once they are in place.
- People who want to be movie stars move to L.A. Those who want to be country music stars move to Nashville. Live in the future you want to create.

THE SECOND COMPONENT OF FOCUS: RESOURCES

Resource allocation is the second component of the Primary Instinct of Focus. The term itself sounds like something you would hear from a financial advisor. And to be sure, effectively allocating your resources does include budgeting and appropriately investing your money. But to your Boss Brain, your most valuable resource isn't money; it's your ability to direct everything at your disposal toward a singular goal.

Your ancestors didn't work to obtain things that held no long-term value. If an item did not regularly create value or contribute to the bigger picture, it was unnecessary. Anything that slowed them down or under-mined their effort to create a better future was left by the wayside. Cer-tainly, this meant sacrificing some small luxuries along the way. Those sacrifices were temporarily painful, but that is the price that must be paid in advance. You are buying the future that you want to create.

Entrepreneurs are generally opportunists. And in this world, there is limitless opportunity to enhance life incrementally. However, optimizing your current conditions is not the goal. It's okay if you want to increase your skills and abilities incrementally over time, but squandering your resources to improve the status quo marginally only perpetuates your existing conditions. It does nothing to bring you closer to your vision of the future.

The resources at your disposal are not just the stuff you have accu-mulated along the way; they are the culmination of your life's work. Your money, network, colleagues, friends, education, and the lessons you have learned are all the result of a lifetime of sweat and sacrifice. If you are not directing the sum of all the work that you have done in your life toward your desired goal, then what was it all for?

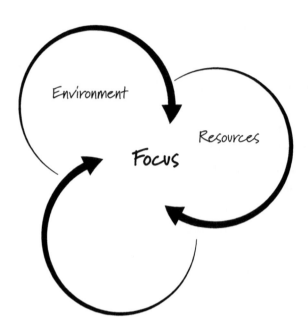

Resources is the second component of the Primary Instinct of Focus

WAYS TO MAXIMIZE YOUR RESOURCES

- Assess the value of everything you own, not in dollars, but as it relates to your entrepreneurial endeavors. If it doesn't meaningfully contribute, then it is a waste of resources.
- Consolidate all the fragmented aspects of your life. Divided resources are less valuable than their collective sum.
- Look for second and third-order resources. These are the things that are not under your control but are available to you nevertheless.
- Shield everything that is at your disposal from interference and encroachment. When you allow others to steal away portions, even unintentionally, you are giving away your future.

THE THIRD COMPONENT OF FOCUS: TIME

Time is the last component of the Primary Instinct of Focus. Many will say that time is a resource, but it is not. Resources hold inherent value.

But unlike actual resources, time holds no value in and of itself. Value is created by how your time is used.

Our forefathers used their time in ways that created the world we live in today. Their vision of the future became a reality in part because of their effective use of time. But we use time differently now. We spend most of it maintaining and enjoying the world that our ancestors created . . . as proven by our dramatically reduced individual productivity. So, what does that mean for our grandchildren and their grandchildren? Collectively, we are likely to regress. But individually, we have the opportunity to soar.

The biggest problem for time management isn't that there aren't enough hours in the day. The biggest problem is that resources are not effectively utilized. Time and money are not the same things, but in today's world, they are inextricably linked. Poverty of wealth creates a poverty of time. Having a large income doesn't automatically generate leisure. If you are burdened with an equivalent amount of debt, then you are just as trapped as anyone else.

Fortunately, at this point, you have belief, accountability, a controlled environment, and appropriately allocated resources to leverage in your quest to redirect how you use your time. You need all those things to yield discretionary hours that can be directed toward your business. This is why recapturing time is so far along within the entrepreneurial process. You cannot just wake up one day and conjure more time; you need a controlled environment and appropriately allocated resources to generate those hours.

In the end, you can use your resources to buy temporary rewards, or you can use them to buy time and your future. It is a matter of choice.

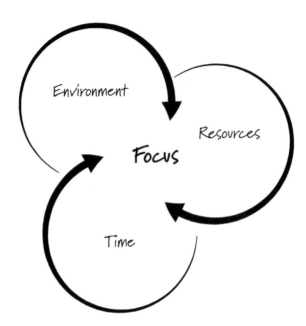

Time is the third component of the Primary Instinct of Focus

WAYS TO GENERATE DISCRETIONARY TIME

- Calculate the value of leveraged tech. Are you more productive or more complacent because of it? Redirect the time it yields or lose it forever. Spend dollars to save hours, not hours to save dollars.
- Calculate your income per hour and assess whether you would pay someone that amount for the time it takes to complete your weekend to-do list. If not, then change your circumstances because you are undervaluing your time.
- Commit to using credit wisely or not at all.
- Research and get to know all the funding options that are available to you. These second and third-order resources can free up huge chunks of your time.
- Have the courage to examine your current finances honestly. Remember that most purchases do not increase the likelihood of reaching your goals.

INTENSE FOCUS

Environment, resources, and time maintain the Primary Instinct of Focus. The word focus is usually used to describe brief periods of intense concentration, like driving in heavy rain or doing a math problem. But to your Boss Brain, focus is much more than quick moments of targeted attention. It is your baseline state of existence.

Focus is the result of eons of evolution, choosing exactly where and how to apply effort. Without it, your energy is wasted. Mother Nature did not design you to chase shiny things across the parking lot. If she had, the human species would have quickly gone extinct. This means that every single distraction you fall victim to is a manmade creation. Every fleeting pleasure and self-serving reinforcement is a fiction that temporarily changes how you feel about yourself but does not permanently advance your future.

For entrepreneurs, like everyone else, your focus is your reality. If your environment, your resources, and your time are not all directed toward the same goal, then at least some part of them is wasted. And while you can always reshape your environment and regain lost resources, lost time is gone forever.

It is the age-old enigma: you have all the fears of a mortal and all the desires of an immortal. However, overcoming your fears doesn't yield focus. That only happens when you limit your desires and delay gratification. You must narrow your focus—from all the things you want, to the one thing that you want *most*. Ignore common impulses for instant gratification and instead focus on the next step within your process. When you focus on the smaller task at hand and ignore distractions, your environment is constantly re-manufactured, and the cycle is perpetuated.

To maintain intense focus, all three components are required.

- You can focus your environment without focusing your resources.
- You can focus your environment and your resources without using your time effectively.
- You only reshape your future only when you focus your environment, resources, and time.

FOCUS AND FIREPLACES

The word *focus* likely originated from one of two different root sources. Old Armenian and Latin both used the term to reference a hearth or a fireplace. In ancient times, the fireplace was the focal point in a home. It was the place where everything converged; it was where you warmed yourself, cooked, spent time with family, and read. As disconnected as the words seem at first, calling a fireplace a focus makes a lot of sense.

In ancient Sanskrit, the term had a different meaning: *to shine*. Unlike being the point where everything converged, the Sanskrit word referenced the point where light is emitted, the source that allows us to see all that we see. It also makes perfect sense to say that to shine is to focus.

We live in a world without focus. Everyone is pulled in a thousand different directions. We constantly divert our attention from one place to another. There is never a focal point. Cooking, reading, and spending time with family are now what we do after our attention has been exhausted. But to our ancestors, who created the word focus, these were the focal points of life.

To the entrepreneur, focus is both the point where our attention originates and converges. It is both how we see and what we see. Entrepreneurial eyes see what everyone else is looking at in a different way. They see things differently because entrepreneurial eyes are different. They shine on what matters most, the point where everything converges.

Entrepreneurs who are not yet focused should carefully eliminate distractions from their environment and thoughtfully allocate their money and other resources. You can manage your daily schedule more easily when resources are abundant and when distractions are scarce. Only then can you choose to spend your time in intrinsically valuable ways. Or, like Napoleon, you can squander a third of your resources and wait for the ground to dry.

PART IV: THE LIES WE ARE TOLD

CHAPTER 13

IT WASN'T MEANT TO BE

> "THE ONLY PERSON YOU ARE DESTINED TO BECOME IS
> THE PERSON YOU DECIDE TO BE."
> –Ralph Waldo Emerson

As a rule, people want to do things that give them the most information about their competence. Tasks that are incredibly easy or insanely difficult are quickly abandoned. If the perceived probability or value of success is too low, then the brain loses motivation. However, if the difficulty is moderate, and a person feels like their decisions are a major factor in the probability of success, motivation and persistence increase. In a motivational sense, moderately difficult tasks are more alluring than very easy or very hard tasks because they provide feedback about our abilities. We try harder when our skills determine the outcome. It is a self-serving motivational bias, and nowhere is it more evident than in the video gaming world.

If a game is too hard, the probability of success is too low. If the game is too easy, the value of success is too low. A game is most fun when the odds are about even, and the player's skill increases each time the game is played. The probability of success, therefore, also increases, and the player becomes intrinsically motivated. Ultimately, this leads to greater persistence.

In addition to ego satiation, progressive difficulty has another addictive quality. It presents a hierarchy of connected short- and long-term goals. Short-term goals have a higher probability but lower value. Long-term goals have lower probability but higher value. When short- and long-term goals are disconnected, motivation decreases. People are more likely to persist and eventually achieve a long-term goal that is related to short-term goals. Conversely, people are more likely to achieve short-term goals that are connected to a meaningful long-term goal. Players will spend hours and hours navigating levels of a game that are progressively more difficult to pursue a distant, highly valued goal.

Sixty-six percent of kids aged eight to 12 play video games for an average of two hours per day, and 56% of teens ages 13 to 17 play video games for an average of 2.5 hours per day. Mastering each level within the game requires constant learning. Pressing one single button will not win the game and offer the reward. The process of achieving the long-term goal requires short-term trial and error and, most importantly, ingenuity.

SELF-EFFICACY AND INGENUITY

Ingenuity is a defining human characteristic. But humans are not the only species with a penchant for innovation. Researchers have documented the capacity in a growing number of other creatures. Some of their findings defy conventional wisdom about the origins and perpetuation of creativity in the human mind.

As the saying goes, invention is born of necessity. Primatologist Carel van Schaik of the University of Zurich has come to a very different view. "When food is scarce, orangutans go into energy-saving mode. They minimize movement and focus on unappealing fallback foods." That strategy is the opposite of innovation. "Trying something new can be risky—you can get injured or poisoned—and it requires a serious investment of time, energy, and attention, while the outcome is always uncertain," van Schaik explains.

Studies of humans faced with food scarcity mirror van Schaik's orangutan findings. In 2013, a Harvard study showed that when sugarcane farmers in India were reminded about their financial struggles, their capacity to think creatively and solve problems in novel situations was reduced. The same sugarcane farmers performed much better on the same test after receiving the once-a-year payment for their produce. A temporary solution to their monetary concerns increased their capacity to think creatively. [1]

Like entrepreneurship, innovation is not born of necessity.

These studies suggest that when the mind is preoccupied with necessities like food, shelter, or money, the capacity to look for and create innovative solutions for long-term problems decreases. Arousal levels, then, directly affect performance. When arousal levels are too low and very predictable, motivation is lost, and complacency sets in. But when arousal is too high, like when our skill level can't change the outcome or when we feel out of control, we lose one of the fundamental aspects of our humanity. We lose ingenuity and the ability to find new ways to enhance our situation. We get stuck in a mental quagmire.

Worry, strife, and a preoccupation with survival shut down our creative abilities.

The idea that suffering inspires innovation flies in the face of scientific research. Worry, strife, and a preoccupation with survival shut down our creative abilities. From the sugarcane farmers of India to the 100 million would-be entrepreneurs currently living in America, when our brains are focused on enduring hardship, we lose the capacity to tap into our innate creativity.

This is one reason why children, who have little preoccupation with basic necessities, are the most creative of us all.

CREATIVE GENIUS

In 1968, George Land conducted a research study to test the creativity of children. He used the same creativity test NASA used to select innovative engineers and scientists. He tested 1,600 children between the ages of three and five. He then re-tested the same children at ten years of age and

---

1. Sendhil Mullainathan and Eldar Shafir, Scarcity: Why Having Too Little Means so Much, New York: Picador, Henry Holt and Company, 2014.

again at fifteen. The results were unprecedented. The proportion of those who scored at the genius level was:

- 98% of five-year-olds
- 30% of 10-year-olds
- 12% of 15-year-olds

Land then tested 280,000 adults with an average age of 31. *Only 2% of the adults scored at genius levels.*

According to Land, there are two types of creative thinking. Convergent thinking is where you judge ideas, consciously criticizing and refining them. And divergent thinking is where new ideas spring from your subconscious.

Land noted that the precipitous drop-off in creative geniuses wasn't genetic or inherent. It was due to a fatal flaw of the education system: we teach and expect children to use both kinds of thinking at the same time. As it turns out, it's impossible to use both simultaneously. Even if we could, research shows that teachers dislike creative students. Teachers reward convergent thinkers more often. Gradually, kids stop thinking creatively, and convergent thinking is selected for success.

As we age, the process continues—pragmatism eventually replaces ingenuity. And when we are stressed, predictability dominates possibility. Like the Sri Lankan farmers who wasted their resources and could not fathom a way out of their situation, stressed employees tend to remain employees. Stress takes away our inherent ability to look for and devise ways to make our lives better. When we are stressed, we become more dutiful and less willing to try new things. In this way, stress is self-replicating—the more stressed you feel, the less likely you are to look for (and try) new ways to escape that feeling.

THE BIAS AGAINST INNOVATION

We herald ingenuity as a cornerstone of innovation and advancement, but we are incredibly resistant to new ideas and change. In fact, researchers have come to question whether society even desires creative ideas. When asked, most business leaders, scientific institutions, and decision-makers tout the importance of new ideas as a driving force behind discovery and positive change. People strongly support the importance of creativity in theory while routinely rejecting creative ideas in reality. Teachers who acknowledge creativity as an important educational goal often dislike students who exhibit curiosity and creative thinking.[2]

New ideas are judged and criticized by the modern brain's thirst for certainty. All new ideas are unproven, and unproven means uncertain. Convergent thinkers immediately doubt if a novel idea is useful. Therefore, it sees novelty and utility as opposites even though every useful innovation was once novel. Practical ideas are subsequently more valued even under pressure to endorse creative ideas.

To make matters worse, the way we evaluate ideas is not necessarily overt. Outward criticism of creativity is a social faux pas. This makes the bias against innovation particularly sinister. To endorse a novel idea is to risk failure, and when 98% of adults are convergent thinkers, the mere expression of a novel idea opens an innovative thinker to social rejection. Society pretends to love and even seek out creativity. But the modern brain's addiction to predictability quickly dismisses novelty, the heart of what makes ideas innovative in the first place.

CREATING REDEMPTION

You have most likely never heard of Edward Bulwer-Lytton. In 1830, he authored the novel *Paul Clifford*. While the novel itself is not widely known or studied, its first line has become the archetype for literary cliché. The novel's opening sentence is, "It was a dark and stormy night; the rain fell in torrents—except at occasional intervals, when it was checked by a violent gust of wind, which swept up the streets . . ."

Writer's Digest described the phrase "it was a dark and stormy night" as the literary poster child for terrible opening lines. However, the *American Book Review* ranked the line as No. 22 on its list of best first lines from novels. The disparity of their opinions reveals both the abundance of and our reverence for creating redemption stories.

---

2. Jennifer Mueller, et al, "The Bias Against Creativity: Why People Desire But Reject Creative Ideas," Psychological Science, 23, 13-7. 10.1177/0956797611421018.

Redemption stories start badly but end better. The lead character inevitably overcomes some "dark and stormy" periods of unfair persecution and then uses the lessons from that triumph to vanquish their persecutor. As we construct a narrative for ourselves, we look for opportunities to paste stories of redemption into our identity and use them to build a legacy: *the time I spent recovering from my car accident made me realize what is important in life, filing bankruptcy was the wakeup call I needed to stop chasing material pleasure and start living with meaning.*

We plug redemption stories into the narrative of our lives like levels in a video game. Each level requires greater skill and contributes directly to the larger arc of our lives as a series of victories over adversity.

One of the most salient aspects of American culture is to redeem yourself in some heroic way and prove yourself worthy of being cloaked in liberty.

Redemption is particularly pervasive in the American narrative. As one researcher put it, "evolving from the Puritans to Ralph Waldo Emerson to Oprah Winfrey . . . Americans have sought to author their lives as redemptive tales of atonement, emancipation, recovery, self-fulfillment, and upward social mobility. The stories speak of heroic individual protagonists—the chosen people—whose manifest destiny is to make a positive difference in a dangerous world . . ."[3]

A redemption story is like a Norman Rockwell painting. It is a stalwart belief in every individual's potential to overcome challenges through hard work, perseverance, and determination. One of the most salient aspects of American culture is to redeem yourself in some heroic way and prove yourself worthy of being cloaked in liberty. Redemption is peak American.

Studies have shown that finding positive outcomes from negative experiences relates to greater life satisfaction. Even when controlling for

3. K.C. McLean, et alK. C., Syed, M., Pasupathi, M., Adler, J. M., Dunlop, W. L., Drustrup, D., . . . Mc-Coy, T. (2019, April 19). "The Empirical Structure of Narrative Identity: The Initial Big Three," Journal of Personality and Social Psychology, 119(4), 920–944. https://doi.org/10.1037/pspp0000247.

general optimism, research shows that having more redemption stories in your narrative correlates with higher well-being. Like any story, though, life stories must be created. It doesn't matter whether you are Tom Hanks marooned on a deserted island or George Orton overcoming a childhood fall; crafting your redemption story requires ingenuity and creativity.

It's not always easy to find patterns and correlations between otherwise unrelated events in your past. Convergent thinkers quickly judge and dismiss loosely connected storylines, but researchers have shown that accuracy isn't always the most important characteristic of life stories. For narrative psychology researchers, "what really matters is whether people are making something meaningful and coherent out of what happened. Any creation of a narrative is a bit of a lie. And some lies have enough truth."

With the right amount of trial and error, stories of entrepreneurship inevitably become redemption stories.

INNOVATION, AMBITION, AND LEGACY

There is social pressure to doubt new and novel ideas. Business ideas are judged especially harshly because of our emotional and volatile relationship with money. The modern brain doesn't actively support creative ventures because they are uncertain. So, the bias against creativity stifles entrepreneurship in two ways: first by undermining innovation, and second, by blurring the lines between ambition and legacy.

Ambition is what you want to achieve for yourself. Legacy is how you impact others. Ambitions are accomplished while legacies are created. There is enormous social pressure to be ambitious, to compete for individual status and wealth. Others may witness your ambition, but they do not necessarily benefit from it. The bias against creativity stifles entrepreneurship by perpetuating blind ambition.

On the other hand, legacies are not about you; they are about your impact on those around you who benefit from your efforts. Legacies are not individual accomplishments to be admired in hindsight. They are expressions of potential, creations that help shape the future of others. A legacy cannot be given to you by an employer because the future isn't shaped by climbing a ladder that someone else built.

Relenting to the bias against innovation is made easier because it is self-serving. You become the primary focus, not others. You can look back on your life and be satisfied with your relative success. You can be happy with what you did and how you did it—the key words being *what* and *how*. This is why innovative business strategies are often quickly dismissed: they focus on who and why when the rest of the world is focused on what and how.

THE HIGH COSTS OF KNOWING

Imagine you are a lion chasing a meerkat that retreats into one of its burrows. Once sheltered, the meerkat must choose how long to wait before emerging. As a hungry lion, you must also choose the length of time for which a meerkat is worth waiting. They are small, after all. And even if it emerges soon, it might run into another burrow before you can catch it. Both of you pay opportunity costs for your persistence. The meerkat cannot forage while hiding, and you cannot hunt for other prey while waiting.

You might think of this waiting game as a war of attrition where the winner is the one that persists the longest. However, the winner in a war of attrition does not pay the full costs of persistence once its opponent surrenders. If the meerkat emerges sooner than your chosen wait time has ended . . . boom. Lunch is served without giving up all the time you were prepared to sacrifice.

By contrast, the meerkat has no way of knowing if you have given up and departed before it emerges. Therefore, live or die, the meerkat always pays the full cost of its chosen wait time. It pays for the need to know if you have left.

Studies have shown that, when faced with this scenario, the predator usually departs immediately.[4] Predators are opportunistic. They don't need to know all the details about this individual meerkat. Before choosing a wait time, an over-analytical lion might weigh relevant facts like this particular meerkat's level of patience, how old it is, or how well fed it is. And the time spent obsessing over those details means less time hunting other prey and, therefore, higher opportunity costs.

---

4. Don M. Hugie, "The waiting game: a 'battle of waits' between predator and prey," Behavioral Ecology, Volume 14, Issue 6, November 2003, pages 807–817.

Just like an over-analytical lion, researchers from the University of Leeds recently revealed how entrepreneurial persistence is affected by the need to know all the facts. The study separated entrepreneurs based on their cognitive thinking styles: knowing, planning, and creating. Individuals with a knowing style prefer facts and details, while a planning style prefers structure and order. Those with a creating style see problems as opportunities.

The study examined the effects of these cognitive styles on the relationship between optimism and persistence. As expected, entrepreneurs with cognitive creating and cognitive planning styles showed great tenacity and persistence. Their thinking styles "enhance the relationship between their inherent optimism and their persistence."[5]

However, there were unexpected findings for those with cognitive knowing style. Entrepreneurs who postpone decisions until all data is collected lose the relative usefulness of their inherent optimism. Their need to collect and weigh all information reduces their ability to convert optimism into action, even after all data is in. Age, gender, and education did not affect entrepreneurial persistence. But the need to know, the need for evidence supporting certainty, weakens the effect of optimism on persistence, and opportunity costs skyrocket.

Ingenuity is the bridge between focused effort and persistence.

Ingenuity is the bridge between focused effort and persistence. Without the need to know all the details, an entrepreneur is free to move forward, experiment, and learn from trial and error.

Immediately abandoning a hiding meerkat might imply that lions have low persistence, but it is the boldest course of action. Without further examination, the lion continues the hunt elsewhere. Lions believe in their ability to create opportunities out of problems, while meerkats pay for the need to know.

---

5. S. Adomako, et al, "Entrepreneurs' Optimism, Cognitive Style and Persistence," International Journal of Entrepreneurial Behaviour and Research, 22 (1). pp. 84-108. ISSN 1355-2554.

WHY DOES THIS MATTER?

Evolution has instilled incredible levels of resourcefulness and ingenuity into each of us. It may not feel like it, but we are the most adaptable species on the planet. One of our greatest gifts is being open to and embracing change. But as we assimilate into society, we lose that creativity and replace it with a preference for simple solutions that are readily available. The struggle to make ends meet heightens our emotions and stifles our instinctive creative abilities making everything feel harder.

As an objective measurement, difficulty does not exist. It is a relative expression of current ability, like the difference between a video game's first and last level. Entrepreneurs must tie easy, short-term goals of lower value to the harder, highly valued cause of building a legacy. Each step taken requires new strategies and creative tactics. A subsequent increase in self-efficacy is the reward for participation, which enhances performance.

In a competitive market with unlimited social mobility, the act of creating a legacy is an atonement for the freedom to do so. Therefore, even without unfair persecution, each step along the way is its own redemption story. But without creativity, ambition is masturbation. It's a self-serving act that does nothing to shape the future.

It is commonly thought that relentless effort within a process is linear, which is the opposite of creative, divergent thinking. Supposedly, creativity is not part of a defined process; it spontaneously springs from some unknown place. That may be true, but it is relentless effort within a process that opens the doors to change and innovative ideas.

Edison famously tried thousands of ways to build a light bulb before succeeding. No doubt his construction and testing process was similar, if not the same, each time. But from within that process sprang new ideas to build and try. There was no Archimedes-type eureka moment.

When challenged, our ancestors became more resourceful and creative. They didn't allow insecurity to squander time or opportunity. However, the modern brain celebrates new and original ideas only after becoming widely accepted and rejects the uncertainty of change. As a result, would-be entrepreneurs convince themselves that if it's not simple and easy, then it wasn't meant to be.

KEY POINTS

- Each one of us was born with inherent, genius-level ingenuity.
- When you are preoccupied with survival, your ability to innovate is limited.
- Society is biased against creative ideas despite touting an explicit preference for them.
- Each step of the entrepreneurial process is itself a redemption story.
- The need to know everything will stop you from doing anything.

QUESTIONS TO ASK

- Do I dismiss ingenious ideas because they are uncertain?
- How can I nurture my ingenuity?
- Am I willing to attempt limitless trials and learn from the errors?
- Am I creating a legacy, or is blind ambition wasting my potential?

CHAPTER 14

IT'S IMPOSSIBLE

"TO BELIEVE A THING POSSIBLE IS TO MAKE IT SO."
—FRENCH PROVERB

The usage frequency of the word *impossible* decreased virtually every year from 1912 to 2000 in the English-speaking world. It's perfectly logical if you examine the events of that year. After all, 1912 was a banner year for achieving the impossible.

On March 1, 1912, U.S. Army Captain Albert Berry was the first man to jump from an airplane with a parachute attached to his back and land safely on the ground. On October 1, 1912, the New York Yankees lost their 100th game of the season. They would eventually finish the season 50-102. And of course, on April 15th, 1912, the unsinkable RMS Titanic struck an iceberg and sank off the coast of Newfoundland. 1912 was truly the year of the impossible.

As mankind steadily advanced through the 20th century, the word's usage continued to decline. After all, only a few decades earlier, no one would have believed that man would soon fly across the Atlantic Ocean, build skyscrapers more than a quarter-mile into the air, split the atom, and walk on the moon. However, in the minds of the 20th centurions, nothing was impossible.

Then, after nearly a hundred years, the word sprang back into usage. In 2001, the word *impossible* inexplicably reached usage levels higher than it had seen in a decade. Steady increases in usage since that time imply an ongoing shift in either the public's perception of what is possible or in the meaning of the word itself.

The timing of the word's resurgence is truly ironic. On Feb 12, 2001, mankind successfully landed a spacecraft on an asteroid 160 million miles from Earth. Only three days later, the first draft of the complete human genome was published. And, of course, on September 11, 2001, hijackers took over three commercial airline flights and destroyed the World Trade Center and part of the Pentagon. 2001 had its fair share of events that proved nothing is impossible. And yet, despite all evidence to the contrary, the word *impossible* was once again spreading like wildfire through English vernacular. After nearly a century of man proving virtually anything is possible, impossible was making a comeback.

What is even more curious is the decade of prosperity that preceded the spike in usage of impossible. The decade began with the collapse of the Soviet Empire. After a half-century, fear of global nuclear Armageddon ceased to exist. From 1990 to 1999, the median American household income grew by 10%. During the 1990s, the Dow Jones industrial average increased by more than 300%. In 1998, the U.S. experienced a federal budget surplus for the first time in 30 years. Unbelievably, surpluses were also recorded in 1999, 2000, and 2001. During this period, there was also a dramatic reduction in violent crime as the murder rate in the United States declined by a whopping 41%.

Nearly every quality of life and positive economic indicator rose for ten years before impossible making its comeback. That is, all but one— entrepreneurship. From 1991 to 2001, self-employment fell from 11% to 9%. The 1990s spawned a perfect environment for business creation: economic expansion, reductions in poverty, decreases in crime, and global stability. But during that time, fewer and fewer would-be entrepreneurs seized the opportunity.

This statistical enigma reveals how the word *impossible* could re-emerge during a time of such prosperity. The more certain we are of our ability to survive, the less likely we are to attempt to flourish. In other words, as the quality of current conditions increases, so does the brain's resistance to change. Just as the second and third generation of the very first farm had a very high probability of survival, so too did the would-be entrepreneurs who remained employees during the 1990s. In their minds, the current conditions simply didn't justify the risk.

We succumb to comforts and safety and respond with complacency. But comfort is a cage that we can live in only by telling ourselves that venturing beyond our line of sight is dangerous or even impossible. Of course, it is not impossible. It's simply that the allure of autonomy and independence doesn't pull quite as hard in times of plenty. Therefore, entrepreneurship doesn't increase because of prosperity; it increases despite it.

GRAVITY AND GOLDILOCKS

In February 2013, a nationwide survey was conducted by two companies: Phillips & Company, a global communications firm, and Explore Mars, a non-profit corporation committed to advancing the cause for human exploration of Mars. The survey measured public perception and levels of support toward human and robotic exploration of the red planet. The poll found that 71% of Americans were confident that humans would go to Mars by 2033. When told that there are currently two operational NASA rovers on Mars, 67% of respondents agreed the U.S. should send both humans and robots to Mars.

Clearly, there is no urgent reason to go to Mars, just like there was no urgent reason to go to the moon. We aren't being *pushed* to go there. Mars might have only one-third the gravity of Earth, but something is pulling us there. Like Mars, the rewards of entrepreneurship pull people in. The allure of self-employment has its own gravity. But not everyone feels that gravity.

Like the hand-to-mouth villagers in Sri Lanka, the more preoccupied we are with survival, the less likely we are to think creatively and innovate new ways to earn income or escape the prison of need. When no other alternative presents itself, people aren't pulled into self-employment—they resort to entrepreneurship; they are pushed there.

On the other end of the spectrum are highly compensated employees. They are very comfortable and live in a safe, predictable environment.

High levels of comfort create an aversion to change. They don't feel pushed or pulled toward entrepreneurship.

Entrepreneurial growth is then least likely among poor populations in time and capital and populations that are rich in time and capital. So, where do the 100 million American would-be entrepreneurs reside? In the middle class.[1]

Studies show that as a country's gross domestic product increases, its level of entrepreneurship decreases.[2] When resources are scarce, business ownership feels impossible. And when harvests are bountiful, starting a new business feels unnecessary. But a place exists somewhere between financial hardship and financial windfall. It is the Goldilocks Zone, where comfort is high enough to invite risk but not certain enough to discourage change. Entrepreneurial growth depends on the people in this Goldilocks Zone. That is why there is a direct correlation between the advancement of the American middle class and the decline of American entrepreneurship. Comfort has stifled our creativity and made us very resistant to change.

A place exists somewhere between financial hardship and financial windfall. It is the Goldilocks Zone, where comfort is high enough to invite risk but not certain enough to discourage change.

BETTING ON THE PAST

The legendary gambler Nick "The Greek" Dandalos once said, "The next best thing to gambling and winning is gambling and losing." It is estimated that he won and lost $500 million during his career—our urge to gamble stretches back to the ancient Egyptians. The Roman emperor Claudius wrote a book about how to win at dice. In fact, gambling was so popular in ancient Rome that the Senate tried to restrict it to Saturdays. But gambling isn't

1. D. Acemoglu, and F. Zilibotti, "Was Prometheus Unbound by Chance? Risk, Diversification and Growth," Journal of Political Economy 105(4): 709–51.

2. Z. Acs and J.E. Amorós, "Entrepreneurship and Competitiveness Dynamics in Latin America," Small Business Economics (31): 305–22.

just an entertaining pastime. For better or for worse, it is an integral part of human success.

Despite the popularity of gambling throughout our history, nobody analyzed the math involved until the Renaissance. Until then, gamblers followed their gut feeling. Even today, the modern brain continues to ignore the math.

Imagine you walk up to a roulette table that has just landed on five red numbers in a row. Would you choose to place your bet on red or black? If you think that black is more likely because it is 'due,' then prepare your modern brain for disappointment. After each spin, most players move their chips around and bet on different numbers. In our guts, we feel that the odds are more in our favor if we try different bets. But each time the wheel is spun, the odds are the same. Changing your bet doesn't change the odds, and the outcome of past spins doesn't predict the outcome of future spins. The wheel has no memory and an infinite number of spins to establish equilibrium.

If you think that starting a successful business is impossible based on past events, you are betting on black because you think it is due. Your past is a subjective narrative that you created to unify random events. Your current narrative didn't determine the likelihood of each of those events occurring. In fact, those events didn't matter until you selected them to be part of your life story. Just because something has never been done doesn't mean it is impossible. Changing your bet doesn't change the odds, and rewriting your past doesn't change the future.

> *Changing your bet doesn't change the odds, and rewriting your past doesn't change the future.*

Entrepreneurs should place their bets while wearing blinders because the outcome of past effort doesn't alter the likelihood of future success. The odds of each attempt depend only on the effort applied within current conditions—or today's bet. Because there is an infinite number of spins in entrepreneurship, previous wins and losses are irrelevant. The only thing that has the power to change the future is what you do in the present.

When you use yesterday to predict tomorrow, you give it power over today.

COMFORT AND FEAR

Dubai's fleet of police cars includes a $2.5 million Bugatti Veyron and a $500,000 Lamborghini Aventador. Dubai is located in the United Arab Emirates—the UAE—and is home to the world's tallest building, artificial indoor ski slopes, lavish hotels, and designer retail centers. Just off the coast are man-made islands configured to look like a map of the world. Each island can be purchased for somewhere between seven million and 1.8 billion.

All Emiratis enjoy benefits from the government that exist nowhere else in the world. These benefits include tax-free income, free high-quality health care, subsidized fuel costs, and very generous government-funded retirement plans. Citizens are also offered access to land to build homes with government-sponsored, interest-free loans. Higher education is also free, even when students study abroad.

The perks of living in the UAE don't stop there. The government gives Emirati men $19,000 when they marry an Emirati woman. Once an Emirati mother has completed 15 years of work, she can retire and receive government-subsidized benefits. In one state, the average age of retirement for women is 45, and 55 for men. If an Emirati man dies with living dependents, the government provides for his widow and children until his daughters are married and his sons find work. When the daughter of a deceased retiree marries, the government gives the newlyweds six times the value of the deceased father's monthly pension as a wedding gift. With the minimum monthly pension being $2,800 per month, the honeymooners get at least $16,800 from the government.

Nine out of 10 Emiratis who work are employed by the government. Government jobs, like everything else, are funded by sales within the country's massive oil reserves. Therefore, government employees enjoy long-term job security and tremendous disposable income. This buffet of benefits has spawned a vast middle class, most of whom rely entirely on the government to provide.

You might think that tax-free income, free healthcare, government-subsidized retirement, and interest-free home loans would inspire many entrepreneurs to leap to self-employment. After all, the UAE even has a fund that provides a one-time debt settlement bailout to entrepreneurs who fail. Khalaf Al Hammadi, director-general of the Abu Dhabi Retirement Pensions and Benefits Fund, even said, "We do not have feelings of fear or insecurities about experiencing a financial crisis, or that one will retire, and the government will not stick to its promises."

Emiratis might not fear a financial crisis, but they do fear one thing more than any other country on the planet: entrepreneurship. A recent worldwide study showed that the UAE has the most fearful would-be entrepreneurs on the planet, with more than six out of 10 citing fear of failure as the main reason for inaction. Only 9% of Emiratis describe themselves as fearless entrepreneurs.[3]

UNCOMFORTABLE AND FEARLESS

On the other end of the spectrum, you'll find the most fearless entrepreneurs. Poland, Portugal, and the U.S. are home to the highest percentage of those who *want* to be self-employed, but none even makes the top 16 for fearlessness. When it comes to fearless entrepreneurship, the U.S. ranks 17th globally, right between Latvia and Mexico. American entrepreneurs are far from fearless.

The most fearless entrepreneurs on the planet live in a society with neither guaranteed retirement nor free high-quality healthcare. They live in a country where one in five citizens doesn't have access to clean water, where more than 20% of the population lives on less than $6/day, and 10% of the people didn't have electricity until the late 1990s. The most fearless entrepreneurs in the world live in Ecuador, making up 30% of the population.

> *America has proven that entrepreneurial spirit is not enough to overcome the fear of uncertainty.*

3. Niels Bosma, et al. "Gem 2019/2020 Global Report," Global Entrepreneurship Monitor viewed at https://www.gemconsortium.org/report/gem-2019-2020-global-report.

Obviously, there are intangible cultural differences that cannot be measured. Each country carries its innate spirit of entrepreneurship. However, America has proven that entrepreneurial spirit is not enough to overcome the fear of uncertainty. Only 14% of Americans listed themselves as fearless in the face of entrepreneurship. America has been snared by the same trap that was laid in Jericho 12,000 years ago.

The stark contrast between the UAE and Ecuador reveals a counterintuitive truth about the Goldilocks Zone and entrepreneurial effort. Risk aversion and energy conservation don't rule only in times of scarcity. It also governs when rewards are plentiful and consistent.

Ecuadorians have enjoyed a significant increase in quality of life in the past twenty-five years. So far, they have not allowed an increase in their quality of life to topple them from the peak of fearless entrepreneurialism.

QUALITY AND QUANTITY

In 1921, the idiosyncratic economist Frank Knight finally formalized the distinction between risk and uncertainty in his book *Risk, Uncertainty, and Profit*. Knight saw the world as ever-changing. Fortunately, an ever-changing world constantly brings forth new opportunities for businesses to make profits. But constant change also means we have no way to predict outcomes of future efforts. Knight wrote that the word *risk* applies to situations where we cannot anticipate the outcome of effort, but we can accurately measure the odds. On the other hand, uncertainty is when we do not have all the necessary information to accurately access the odds in the first place, regardless of what is being risked.

A Gallup study recently showed that most would-be entrepreneurs don't understand the difference between uncertainty and risk. The study concluded that increased quality of life leads to lower rates of entrepreneurship around the world. Gallup compared per capita gross domestic product with the self-employment ratio of the population in 135 countries. The study discovered a negative and linear relationship between GDP and self-employment rates. In other words, entrepreneurship is lower in rich countries than in poor ones.[4] But broad measures

---

4. "Country Data Set Details," Gallup viewed at https://www.gallup.com/services/177797/country-data-set-details.aspx.

like gross domestic product are not the only metrics with a relationship to self-employment.

Income data from the U.S. Bureau of Economic Analysis shows a similar pattern. From 1977 to 2011, per capita income in the U.S. increased by 79%. Over the same period, the number of new businesses founded each year declined 49%.[5] That is, as citizens of the United States became wealthier, entrepreneurship declined.

The results of these studies should serve as a cautionary tale for policymakers. Economic development officials want to believe that entrepreneurship is the key to the growth of their local economy. New business startups certainly create jobs, which is always a good thing for economic development. But there is an inverse relationship between a city's quality of life and business formation. When quality goes up, comfort goes up. As per capita income increases, self-employment decreases. As quality rises, so too does the fear of uncertainty.

Increased quality of life and higher incomes widen the entrepreneurship gap. Metro areas then become dependent on increased consumerism to drive economic growth. Existing businesses must expand for the local economy to expand. Increased consumerism means more jobs, and more jobs mean lower levels of entrepreneurship. It is a vicious and self-perpetuating cycle that can be found all over the world because most would-be entrepreneurs don't understand the difference between uncertainty and risk.

There is obviously no certainty in uncertainty, but there is certainty in risk. A person who bets $5 on number 15 at the roulette table cannot know the outcome, but the risk and odds are certain—the probability is 36 out of 37 to lose $5. In this instance, there are clearly defined odds with certainty of what is at risk.

Dr. Weiner's attribution theory from Chapter 5 simply put an entrepreneurial edge on Knight's definition. Weiner showed that the longer our efforts persist, the more proficient we become. Persistence results in greater ability, and greater ability results in higher odds of future success. Persistence reduces risk because it enhances your odds even when the outcome is uncertain.

5. Ronald S. Jarmin and Javier Miranda. The Longitudinal Business Database. [Washington, D.C.]: Center for Economic Studies, U.S. Census Bureau, 2002.

WHY DOES THIS MATTER?

Our world is filled with evidence for the power of possible. What we now consider commonplace would have looked like pure sorcery not too long ago. When *Star Trek* debuted in 1966, their communication devices looked conspicuously like flip phones. At the time, it was science fiction. Motorola's first flip phone hit the market 23 years later in 1989 and made the impossible commonplace. Considering the mountain of evidence to the contrary, deeming anything impossible reveals two biases. First, a bias against creativity. And second, a bias against change. Both of these are most prevalent when the quality of life and comfort are most certain.

The entrepreneur must look past the biases of society. Instead, look to your potential. You most likely have the ability to maintain the life you are currently living. But by simply tweaking your cost of living relative to your current income, you can find yourself in the Goldilocks Zone. There you can comfortably invite a little risk. You can try new things and adapt to new ideas. You can abandon fruitless efforts and pursue other opportunities because your environment doesn't define your identity. You can constantly test and revise innovations because your bet is only on the next spin. You may never reach the fearless stage of the Ecuadorians, but that doesn't mean the odds are any different. There are only two possible outcomes for their efforts and yours.

The meerkats of Chapter 13 knew that hiding longer lowers the odds of the lion still waiting for them when they emerge. Although, they do not have enough information to assess the odds accurately. There is no certainty, and their very lives are at risk. Therefore, they wait for prolonged periods even though the lion usually leaves immediately. This is why most casinos have a digital tower at each roulette table showing the results of the past spins. There is no disclaimer to notify bettors that the results of those past spins have no bearing whatsoever on the odds of future spins (because you can only bet on one spin at a time). But the implication is clear—the outcome of past events can predict the outcome of future results, which is complete rubbish.

Entrepreneurs create certainty by clearly establishing the limits that are at risk. The lesson is not to avoid betting. The lesson is to control the size of your entrepreneurial bet because you don't have enough information to know the odds. Tear down the digital tower and refuse to allow random stories from the past to affect current strategy. It's not gambling when you bet on yourself because your effort defines your odds. Sure, you can't lose what you don't bet, but you also can't win without betting.

KEY POINTS

- Adaptability is the catalyst for evolution.
- Deeming an outcome of unknown odds as impossible inherently limits adaptability and increases change aversion.
- Most entrepreneurs emerge from the comfort of the Goldilocks Zone.
- In entrepreneurship, the outcome of past events plays virtually no role in the odds of future outcomes.
- As comfort and predictability increase, so too does fear of entrepreneurship.
- Risk and uncertainty are not the same.

QUESTIONS TO ASK

- How can I move my comfort level into the Goldilocks Zone and invite measured risk?
- Has my quality of life satiated my desire for self-employment, or has it made me temporarily change-averse?
- Will I regret never placing a bet on myself or my abilities?
- How can I change my life to embrace creativity and change better?

CHAPTER 15

GROW UP

"SUCCESS IS TO BE MEASURED NOT SO MUCH BY THE
POSITION THAT ONE HAS REACHED IN LIFE AS BY THE
OBSTACLES WHICH THEY HAVE OVERCOME."
—Booker T. Washington

Everyone knows the first passage in America's Declaration of Independence—that we are endowed by our Creator "with certain Unalienable Rights, that among these are Life, Liberty, and the Pursuit of Happiness." You may not know that Thomas Jefferson took the phrase "pursuit of happiness" from *An Essay Concerning Human Understanding*, written by John Locke, the English philosopher. His essay, along with his other political writings, helped incite the American Revolution. In the passage where he coined the phrase "pursuit of happiness," Locke writes:

> The highest perfection of intellectual nature lies
> in a careful and constant pursuit of true and solid
> happiness . . . and that we mistake not imaginary for real
> happiness, is the necessary foundation of our liberty.
> The stronger ties we have to an unalterable pursuit of

happiness . . . the more are we free from any necessary
determination of our will. (1894, p. 348)

The foundation of liberty is built upon our "careful and constant pursuit" while not mistaking "imaginary for real happiness." To mistake imaginary happiness for real happiness is to deny ourselves the foundation of true liberty. Read in context, Jefferson chose Locke's phrasing to emphasize that real happiness was not something you own or a temporary pleasure. The pursuit of genuine happiness means you are "free of any necessary determination of (y)our will." In other words, free from being told what to do.

Your Boss Brain desires independence and autonomy. Happiness then is in the zealous pursuit of individual achievement, not in attainment. The Founding Fathers recognized this innate human desire, captured its essence in the Declaration of Independence, and protected it in the Bill of Rights. Locke and Jefferson knew that the American Dream was in the freedom to pursue your unique definition of happiness, whatever that may be.

Any attempt to create a utopian society where the collective defines every person's role is optimistic. But it is also in direct conflict with the mental framework that brought us out of the caves and allowed us to occupy virtually every corner of the planet. As Yuval Harari noted in *Sapiens*, "Biology enables, culture forbids."

THE HAPPINESS RIPPLE EFFECT

A popular misconception is that entrepreneurship is rewarding in the long term, but it brings stress and unhappiness in the short term. That is not what studies reveal. Being a business owner is hard, but recent studies show that 81% of independent workers are happier since they became independent, and 60% even report being healthier.[1]

Other studies also reveal that, on average, those who are self-employed are more engaged, more satisfied, and happier with work than traditional

---

1. "America's Independents a Rising Economic Force: State of Independents in America Report," MCO Partners, 2016, viewed at https://www.mbopartners.com/wp-content/uploads/2019/02/2016_MBO_Partners_State_of_Independence_Report.pdf.

employees.[2] Happiness makes us feel good, but it also leads to a wide range of benefits for our performance, health, and relationships. In one study, economists showed different groups of people either a positive film clip or a neutral film clip. They then asked them to carry out standard workplace tasks. The people who were primed to feel happy were 11% more productive than their peers, even after controlling for age, IQ, and other factors.

Similarly, another study found that companies with happy team members outperform the stock market year on year, and a team at UCLA has discovered that people who are happy as young adults go on to earn more than their peers later in life. Happiness directly affects productivity, wealth, and performance.

All evidence points to entrepreneurs living longer, happier lives and their happiness translating into safer, more harmonious societies.

Happiness also has a profound effect on society as a whole. Hundreds of studies have found clear evidence that happier people have better overall health and live longer than their unhappy peers. Happy people are half as likely to catch a common cold, and they have a 50% lower risk of heart attack or stroke.

The most significant argument for the importance of entrepreneurship is that those who pursue happiness are more likely to make a positive contribution to society. Happy people participate in public and civic activities more frequently, and they have greater respect for law and order. Not surprisingly, they are also more likely to volunteer their time to help others.

And as if all the happiness and productivity that entrepreneurship brings wasn't enough, entrepreneurs typically give 50% more to charity than traditionally employed people. Specifically, entrepreneurs donate roughly $1,200 more to charitable causes than traditional employees at the same income level.

---

2. "Work-life 3.0: Understanding how we'll work next," Price Waterhouse Coopers viewed at https://www.pwc.com/us/en/industry/entertainment-media/publications/consumer-intelligence-series/assets/pwc-consumer-intellgience-series-future-of-work-june-2016.pdf.

All evidence points to entrepreneurs living longer, happier lives and their happiness translating into safer, more harmonious societies. Pursuing and attaining happiness as a measure of societal well-being is not some lofty, naïve ideology held by the narrow-minded. It is literally written into the U.S. Constitution. It's the very foundation of creating a more productive, healthy, and cohesive society.

MEANING OR HAPPINESS

Can life be meaningful yet unhappy? Conversely, can life be happy and still lack meaning? Aristotle said that happiness is the meaning and the purpose of life, the whole aim, and end of human existence. Buddhism describes happiness as an optimal state of being, not a mere pleasurable feeling or fleeting emotion. But according to cognitive psychologist and Nobel Prize winner Daniel Kahneman, happiness is a spontaneous and fleeting experience. Kahneman proposes that we desire satisfaction with our lives, which leads in a completely different direction than the maximization of happiness. In his opinion, happiness is brief, but satisfaction is a long-term feeling acquired over time and based on achieving goals and building a life you admire:

> Happiness feels good in the moment. But it's in the moment. What you're left with are your memories. And that's a very striking thing—that memories stay with you, and the reality of life is gone in an instant. So memory has a disproportionate weight because it's with us. It stays with us. It's the only thing we get to keep.

Like Kahneman, the 19th-century philosopher Friedrich Nietzsche felt that it is impossible to determine if our lives have meaning while living. Therefore, the question can't be answered in real time. Memory then is the lynchpin to satisfaction because satisfaction is measured in retrospect. Happiness, however, occurs in real time.

Kahneman found that most of us tell ourselves a story about our lives mostly based on comparison. And even years of positive, fleeting experiences may not necessarily add up to a meaningful story. Ultimately, positive feelings pass while memories endure. Kahneman says that in hindsight, "life satisfaction is connected to social yardsticks—achieving goals, meeting expectations."

Comparisons, competition, social yardsticks, meeting expectations—this explains our current social media-driven culture. We work hard to present the *appearance* of an enviable existence. We post pictures to show everyone how happy we are, while seven in 10 want to quit their jobs. We're preoccupied with signaling status and wealth, while fewer and fewer take control of their financial future each year. This is precisely why Kahneman doubts whether we even want to be happy in the first place. We spend so much time working for a result that is "satisfactory" by comparison that we never do what would make us happy. We say that we want to be happy, but we don't spend our time working toward a life of happiness. So, we waste our whole lives trying to measure up to someone else's expectations. At the end, the sum of our existence is relative anyway. And this story we are telling ourselves, at least according to Kahneman, does not have a happy ending.

Logically, you could lead a meaningful life by sacrificing your happiness for some greater good. What makes a life meaningful is fundamentally distinct from what makes a life happy. The problem is, just like Locke and Jefferson, we tend to think of happiness as a destination and meaning as a virtue. Even though one can be experienced only in real time, and the other can be assessed only in hindsight.

MONEY AND HAPPINESS

Everyone has heard the saying "money can't buy happiness." As a child, did you ever say, "When I grow up, I want to own the things that society has designated are the hallmarks of success?" As a child, you saw material trappings as metaphors for the experiences you wanted to live. We may have dreamed of material things, but those things were usually tools to facilitate an experience or convey meaning. A large yacht was really a medium to sail the oceans. A private plane was merely a metaphor for spontaneous travel. To an eight-year-old, a fancy car doesn't symbolize wealth; it symbolizes freedom and autonomy.

As childhood fades, we are struck by the realization that those things are not a necessary means to our ends. They are icons that represent larger and more personal experiences that cannot be purchased. As adults, those icons ironically become the anchors that prevent us from living those experiences. As Kahneman observed, we live as if being happy is less important than presenting an enviable appearance to others, making us feel more satisfied. Signaling success as society defines it becomes more important than experiences or lifestyles that imbue sustained and lifelong happiness.

Scientific research has shown that happiness increases proportionately with income up to roughly $80,000 per year. After that, the proportionate increase in personal happiness rises by only a fraction with increased wealth. The same study found that $200,000 per year represented the outer edge of the money-happiness connection. After that, there was no positive impact. The connection between money and happiness flattens at the point where our basic needs of food, shelter, and subsistence are met. In other words, if you can afford the basic necessities, you're probably as happy as the world's wealthiest people.

> *If you can afford the basic necessities, you're probably as happy as the world's wealthiest people.*

When subjects were asked whether they felt happy yesterday, income became even less important. The percentage of people who said "yes" to being happy yesterday stops around $50,000, not $80,000. Beyond 50k, income had no meaningful relationship with day-to-day happiness. Even people with a net worth of over 25 million don't show significant increases in happiness.

SOCIAL YARDSTICKS

Ancient Inuit wisdom captured an idea centuries before Thoreau made it famous: enough is plenty. True for most things, but we are not conditioned to think of money in terms of enough. Have you ever said, "If I had a job making $x/year, I would be so happy!"? Then you reached that goal and found out that you still needed more money? The scientific name for this hamster wheel is the hedonic treadmill or hedonic adaptation. We must make more and more money to keep our level of happiness in the same place. Dr. Daniel Crosby describes this phenomenon in his book *You're Not That Great*, which sets forth seven counterintuitive truths for living a meaningful life:

> What tends to happen is that our expectations rise and fall with our earnings, keeping our happiness at a relatively stable place. In much the same way, we tend to project forward to a hypothesized happier time, when we have more money in the bank or are making a bigger salary. The fact of the matter is, when that day arrives, we are unlikely to recognize it and will simply project forward once again, hoping in vain that something outside of ourselves will come and make it all better.

For the entrepreneur, the hedonic treadmill eliminates both meaning and happiness. It destroys meaning by wasting time and resources. It prevents happiness by handcuffing the entrepreneur to the maintenance of debt and existing conditions. More possessions mean more obligations and less freedom. More possessions then dull the pain of less freedom. It's a vicious cycle.

For the entrepreneur, the hedonic treadmill eliminates both meaning and happiness.

According to the author of *Finding Meaning in an Imperfect World*, people who feel their lives are meaningless often fail to recognize what truly matters:

> Many did not pose relevant questions that might have changed their views or take the actions that might have improved their condition. Most of the people who complained about life's meaninglessness even found it difficult to explain what they took the notion to mean.

The problem originates in two ways. First, as Kahneman says, we assess meaning only in retrospect, so we focus our attention on the past. We look at awards, merit badges, and trophies as achievements. Second, we falsely think of legacy as wealth, as some dollar amount, home size, or another material metric. Combined, the misguided arrogance of these two mistakes serves as blinders. We lose sight of what matters and become overly focused on what we believe is missing from our lives. And no amount is ever enough.

We see others who have things we think will bring us happiness, so materialism becomes our vocation. However, you'll always find yourself right where you started, no matter how long you run on the hedonic treadmill.

WHY DOES THIS MATTER?

The Constitution protects Americans' right to liberty and the pursuit of happiness, but the phrase itself implies that happiness is a destination that lies beyond your current situation. And even though you have every opportunity to exercise that right, most fail to find creative ways to initiate their zealous pursuit. Even in the freest country in the world, traditional employment controls nearly every aspect of your life. Of course, entrepreneurs also work long, hard hours and are obligated in perhaps more ways than employees. But there is one distinct difference: entrepreneurs are pursuing the future that they envision for themselves. They are not restrained by anything other than their willingness to fight for what they want. Happiness comes in the zealous pursuit of a dream, not in the attainment.

Admittedly, happiness is transient, but only because we aren't working toward a meaningful legacy. We are working toward what Locke called imaginary happiness. Real happiness is the by-product of the freedom to pursue your unique definition of a meaningful life, whatever that may be.

Your Boss Brain evolved in a world without expectations or limitations. Whatever it could imagine, it could attempt without fear of judgment or banishment. Even though America was founded on entrepreneurship, modern culture now sees the very act as one of rebellion. So, society tells you to grow up and stop dreaming.

The Boss Brain doesn't measure itself against the accomplishments of others or society's definition of success. It doesn't measure meaning in retrospect. Meaning is found in building a legacy. And legacy is determined not by assessing the past but by shaping the future.

KEY POINTS

- Happiness is not a destination that you journey toward. It is the by-product of the freedom to zealously pursue a meaningful life.
- Society's definition of success is what our forefathers called imaginary happiness.
- There was joy in pursuing the original American Dream regardless of your results. Our ancestors found joy in the challenge, not in the reward.
- A meaningful life can only be judged in hindsight, but the freedom to pursue it yields happiness in real time.

QUESTIONS TO ASK

- Have I exercised my right to pursue my definition of happiness?
- What is the first thing I need to do to step off the hedonic treadmill?
- What does my idea of a legacy look like?
- Can I withstand the judgment of others when I embark on self-employment?

CHAPTER 16

THE FOURTH PRIMARY INSTINCT

"THE CREATIVE ADULT IS THE CHILD WHO SURVIVED."
—URSULA LEGUIN

THE FOURTH PRIMARY INSTINCT: CREATIVITY

If anyone can survive adrift and alone on the Atlantic, it is Steve Callahan. He is a lifelong sailor who has lived aboard, raced, and cruised boats of all shapes and sizes. He has studied books on surviving at sea. Steve owns all the correct survival gear and has even practiced how to get off a sinking boat as fast as possible. All that preparation served him well in 1981 when his boat collided with a whale and sank just off the Canary Islands.

Callahan escaped in an inflatable life raft. Once his supplies ran out, he caught and ate fish, barnacles, and even birds. As he drifted westward with the trade winds, Callahan said he survived by "learning to live like an aquatic caveman." He became part of an ecosystem that evolved and followed him for more than 2,000 miles across the Atlantic.

While adrift, Steve spotted nine ships, but none saw him. He knew from the beginning that he could not count on rescue and that he had to rely upon himself. He genuinely believed in his ability to survive the ordeal. Some might have floated aimlessly, feeling powerless to change their fate, but Steve made use of his time. During the day, he exercised and fished. He constantly focused on improving the little survival systems he built with his limited supplies. He then improvised ways to capture more food and water. He navigated by the stars and marveled at their beauty, describing the night sky as "a view of heaven from a seat in Hell."

After 76 days adrift, fishermen plucked Steve from his raft just off the shores of Guadeloupe. During his time adrift, he overcame encounters with sharks, equipment failure, raft punctures, dehydration, starvation, and madness. He holds the record for the longest anyone has survived alone and adrift on the open ocean.

To survive his ordeal, Steve experimented with new ideas; he remained open to any kind of change that might increase his odds of survival, and he found joy in refining his little survival systems. For Steve, there was never a clear, linear path to survival. He faced different challenges minute by minute, and each required a creative solution. To tap into and best utilize his innate creativity, Steve had to do three things: he had to relentlessly try new things and learn from what didn't work. He had to adapt and be open to significant change no matter how far-fetched. And he had to enjoy overcoming the small challenges that lead to the larger goal.

Ingenuity and adaptability are not enough. Unbridled creativity also requires a zealous pursuit, finding joy in the challenge.

THE FIRST COMPONENT OF CREATIVITY: INGENUITY

Ingenuity is the first component of the Primary Instinct of Creativity. Entire eras in our history are dedicated to this way of thinking. Some of the most influential thinkers and philosophers emerged during the Age of Enlightenment and the Renaissance. Today, however, divergent thinkers are often shunned, and their ideas are dismissed.

Since the Industrial Revolution, society has praised and rewarded linear thought and process optimization. But none of that would be needed or even possible if new ideas were not being generated. Our collective rise has created an abundance that enables you to embrace diverse and original perspectives. But simultaneously, the certainty provided by your self-imposed systems silently undermines your acceptance of new ideas.

Life essentials are widely available in America, so we rarely suffer from limited thinking due to scarcity. However, through our prosperity, society still smothers diverse viewpoints and the ability to see the world from a different perspective. Your instinct to innovate is locked up by all the stress and blind ambition spawned by the need for social acceptance and status.

Your ancestors would set goals and then figure out how to reach them. Their willingness to try new things and conjure solutions along the way instilled the confidence they needed to set out into the unknown. Today, without a clear and straight line of sight that leads directly to your goals, you are afraid to take even a single step.

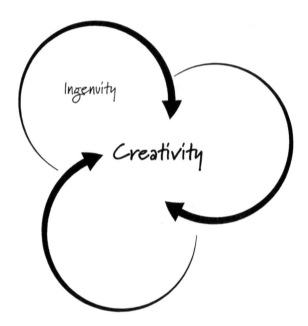

Ingenuity is the first component of the Primary Instinct of Creativity

WAYS TO NURTURE YOUR INGENUITY

- Leverage your network. The best ideas often come from people who are not so close to a project that they can't see it objectively.
- Consciously separate blind ambition from your ultimate goal. Climbing a ladder that someone else built does not require divergent thinking . . . entrepreneurship does.
- Create detailed plans for short-term survival, so your mind is free to innovate long-term solutions.

- Take the first step without the need to know where the second step will lead. Mother Nature gave you what you need to figure it out along the way.

THE SECOND COMPONENT OF CREATIVITY: ADAPTABILITY

Adaptability is the second component of the Primary Instinct of Creativity. Unlike every other animal on this planet, humans now thrive in every environment. We are supremely adaptable. Although, adaptability is often associated with a lack of commitment in today's world as if a willingness to change direction is somehow a character flaw. It is eminently ironic that we now reject change since our modern life was created by embracing it. It is a sad commentary on our future that we have become resistant to the one thing that contributed so much to our success as a species.

Your world and all the things in it are the innovative results born from a willingness to change and evolve. But the certainty provided by centuries of innovation silently undermines your acceptance of new ideas. If you want your future to look different from your present, you have to change your life. If you want to leave a legacy that lasts longer than your life, you have to change the lives of others. It's like a math problem—if you don't change a variable, you cannot expect a different result.

In business and nature, adaptability means survival. Business landscapes change. Markets change. Customer preferences change. If you are unable or refuse to evolve with them, your business will suffer the same fate as every other species with that problem: extinction.

Fortunately, adaptability is your baseline frame of reference. You don't have to become adaptable. Deep down, you already are. You just have to overcome the uncertainty that comes with all new ideas. Change is inevitable. If you embrace it, you can exact some measure of control over it. If you reject it, change will still happen and render your way of thinking obsolete.

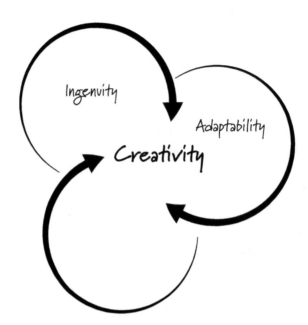

Adaptability is the second component of the Primary Instinct of Creativity

WAYS TO LEVERAGE YOUR ADAPTABILITY

- Test ideas in small ways with clearly defined risk. Revise and test again until the odds are measurable.
- Calculate the tangible resources needed to move into the Goldilocks Zone. Once you are there, adaptability isn't a burden.
- Resisting massive changes that are inevitable is a recipe for extinction. Dealing with disruptive ideas doesn't make you adaptable—it reveals your innate adaptability.
- Do not allow unexpected change to halt your evolution. Times of transition are the perfect backdrop for experimentation.

THE THIRD COMPONENT OF CREATIVITY: ZEAL

A joyful and zealous pursuit is the last component of the Primary Instinct of Creativity. It took only 200 years for America to rise and only 60 years for American entrepreneurship to fall. Somewhere along the way, the happiness that came from the freedom to passionately pursue your full potential was lost. The truth is, your freedoms were lost—not in reality, only in your mind. As you caged them, you caged yourself.

The modern brain is so preoccupied with its relative performance and social status that it willingly gave up happiness to create the appearance of an enviable existence. We stopped looking for ingenious ways to explore our potential and started measuring our success through the eyes of others. But there is no joy in that pursuit.

Trudging your way up through corporate and social hierarchies doesn't require that you be happy. But entrepreneurship does. You must find joy in the process of figuring things out. You have to be motivated by the opportunity to conjure creative ideas and find unique solutions to unexpected problems. Every time you rise to meet adversity head-on, you learn more about your limits. Adversity isn't fun for anyone. But to the entrepreneur, finding out what you are really made of must be.

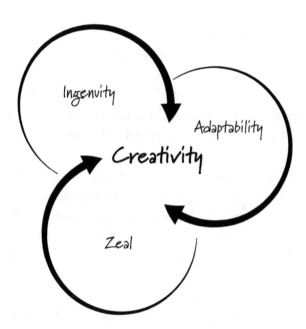

Zeal is the third component of the Primary Instinct of Creativity

WAYS TO BE ZEALOUS

- Accept that happiness is not a destination. It is the by-product of exercising the freedom to pursue meaning and legacy.
- Incorporate your short- and long-term goals into everything you do. Every action should shape your future in some way.

◆ Remember that others will dismiss the creative solutions you
   implement to achieve your goals. When people who love being
   traditionally employed start questioning what you are doing and
   why you are probably on the right track.

◆ Treat each challenge like a scavenger hunt. Zeal comes from
   knowing that the solution you are looking for is out there
   somewhere; you just have to find it.

UNBRIDLED CREATIVITY

Ingenuity, Adaptability, and Zeal maintain the Primary Instinct of Creativity. Mother Nature didn't give us genius-level creativity so we could
paint on the walls of caves. It was and still is a crucial element in our
success. The non-linear nature of our collective rise required on-the-spot
solutions and constant improvisation.

The word creativity is usually reserved for artists and musicians. That
is true if you consider rocket scientists to be artists and the sounds of
drones to be music. That's because there is only one difference between
traditional creativity and modern innovation—the former expands our
thinking, and the latter expands our world. But one cannot exist without
the other.

The Bauhaus movement rightly recognized that the division between
science and art was hindering both. Part of embracing your instinctive
creativity is letting go of what is customary and traditional. That's because
creativity isn't always about what you add; sometimes it's about what
you take away. But your ingenuity and adaptability are useless without
genuine zeal.

As an aspiring entrepreneur, you must embrace the divergent side
of your mind that houses your inherent ingenuity. Be open to all those
ideas that spring from the depths of your brain. Use them as you adapt
to unforeseen challenges. To have zeal is to be energetic, passionate, and
enthusiastic. To be a zealot is to be fanatical, maniacal, and devoted.
When you are zealous, you find joy and fulfillment in the process of
adapting and innovating. That reignites your ingenuity, and the cycle is
perpetuated.

To maintain unbridled creativity, all three components are required.

+ You can have ingenuity without adaptability.
+ You can have ingenuity and be adaptable without having a genuine zeal for entrepreneurship.
+ Your future is only reshaped when you leverage your inherent ingenuity and adaptability with a genuine, zealous pursuit of entrepreneurship.

TRAVEL AND VODKA

Mark Twain was perhaps America's most witty, creative, and sarcastic writer. Although, like all sarcasm, his facetious quips often carried a vein of truth. He once famously remarked that "travel is fatal to prejudice, bigotry, and narrow-mindedness." Anyone who has traveled extensively knows the power of leaving one's little corner of the Earth and seeing cultural diversity firsthand.

Nothing broadens the mind more than travel. It opens the traveler to new ideas and customs that might otherwise be dismissed. However, geography does not open one's mind. It is the physical act of seeing the world from another person's perspective that brings about open-mindedness. Being open-minded allows you to channel your instinctive creativity.

We all crave the relaxed feeling that comes from being open to new ideas and suggestions. Just like happy hour at your local pub, perspective is a social lubricant. But without some catalyst, like travel or vodka, we are much more likely to remain steadfast in our views and opinions.

To be released from the grip of what is customary and tap into their innate creativity, entrepreneurs must separate their prejudice against non-conventional ideas from their self-perception. It is an understand-able bias. After all, if we attempt something in a way that is inconsistent with who we think we are, failure implies both lack of ability and loss of identity. But strategy, however, is useless if we allow our self-perception to limit the variety of our tactics.

The power of creativity is compounded by change. Change is a force multiplier. Each new tactic spawns a dozen previously hidden opportunities. Entrepreneurs must view significant change in strategy as the first step toward significant change in outcome. Trial and error will determine your tactics, but once you've found a tactic that works, use it to refine your entire strategy.

The flow of creative ideas yields new opportunities. Those opportunities, in turn, present new challenges to overcome, requiring more creative ideas. When you find joy in this never-ending cycle, each stage of entrepreneurship carries its own intrinsic value. Without that joy, being an entrepreneur is like floating adrift on the open ocean and being powerless to change your fate.

CHAPTER 17

THE CYCLE OF ENTREPRENEURSHIP

"YOU SHOULD BE FAR MORE CONCERNED WITH
YOUR CURRENT TRAJECTORY THAN WITH YOUR
CURRENT RESULTS."
—JAMES CLEAR, *ATOMIC HABITS*

For 190,000 years, our Boss Brain flourished by moving with and anticipating the cycles of nature. Like every other animal, we found certainty in the changing seasons. Every ending was a new beginning. Birth, death, and rebirth were as inevitable as the sunrise. We found comfort in Mother Nature's predictability. We could always count on her to bring spring thaws and summer bounties. Then, we made a sudden shift. Life became linear.

We are now obsessed with straight lines. Straight highways, straight fences, straight buildings. *Get straight to the point. Be straight with me. Let's get one thing straight. She's talented and going straight to the top.* This is how we see our lives now—as a linear journey from point A to point B. We even rewrite the stories of our lives to form the straightest path to our current situation.

Because of this obsession with all things linear, we now view our collective history as behind us and our future in front of us. We ignore how our own biases and lack of self-awareness cause history to repeat itself over and over again. The modern brain moves on an imaginary pathway that leads in one direction as if our cultural and social evolution also represents biological progress. It's logical to look at our recent technological prowess and assume that we are smarter than our ancestors. And, for the most part, that's true.

For virtually the entire period in which we have measured human intelligence, the average IQ has risen by about three points a decade—a phenomenon known as the Flynn Effect. The steady uptick has lasted for decades. But recent research has yielded frightening news: the trend has reversed.[1]

In the past three decades, the average IQ has fallen by more than seven points, a rate equal to its previous ascent. Our journey is no longer linear. Our trajectory has changed. That is, we can no longer claim to be collectively smarter than previous generations.

Scientists concede the possibility of an ebb and flow within our brains, where intelligence rises and falls over time. Ebbs and flows, beginnings and ends, death and rebirth. It seems even the development of our brains flows in a cycle.

The Four Primary Instincts of the Boss Brain also flow within a cycle—the Cycle of Entrepreneurship. They flow like the changing of the seasons. Each one is useless without the next.

1. Bernt Bratsberg and Ole Rogeberg, "Flynn effect and its reversal are both environmentally caused," Proceedings of the National Academy of Sciences, Jun 2018, 115 (26) 6674-6678; DOI: 10.1073/pnas.1718793115.

B E L I E F : Our optimism and self-efficacy drive our actions. However, that instinct alone was not enough. If we think that variables outside of our control limit us, then they do limit us. Belief means nothing if we feel controlled by the world around us. So, a second instinct was required.

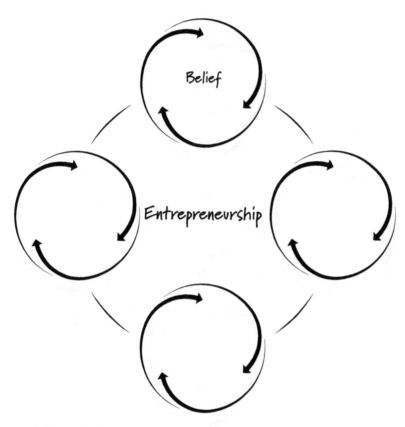

Belief is the first Primary Instinct in the Cycle of Entrepreneurship

ACCOUNTABILITY: To harness the power of belief, we needed to feel in control. Feeling empowered inspired us to create systems and processes. Working within those processes required diligence. So, Mother Nature wired us to be accountable. However, accountability means nothing if progress is mired in distraction. So, a third instinct was required.

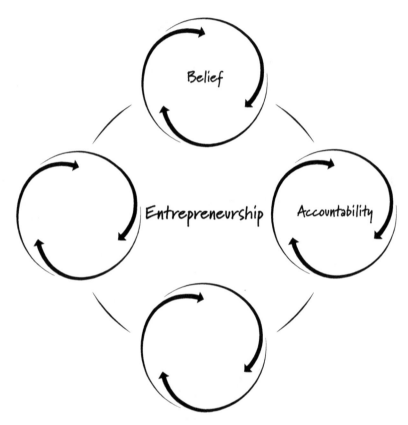

Accountability is the second Primary Instinct in the Cycle of Entrepreneurship

F O C U S : To maximize our accountability, we needed focus—the ability to direct our attention and efforts toward a singular outcome. So, Mother Nature wired us to ignore distractions and direct all our resources and time toward our goals. Along the way, we encountered lots of unforeseen challenges. So, a fourth and final instinct was required to complete the cycle.

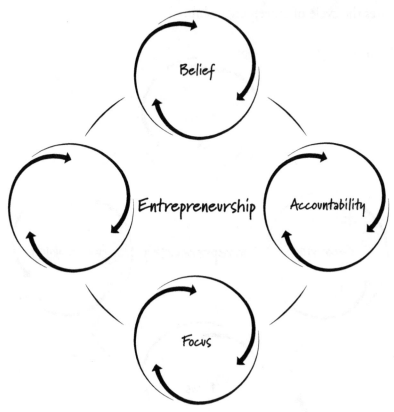

Focus is the third Primary Instinct in the Cycle of Entrepreneurship

CREATIVITY: To overcome the inevitable and unexpected challenges we encountered, we needed creativity—the ability to open our minds and find unique solutions to problems. So, Mother Nature gifted us with genius-level creativity from birth. Our optimism and self-confidence are preserved by our ability to look for and find creative solutions to every obstacle in our path. Therefore, our creativity fuels our belief and perpetuates the cycle of entrepreneurship.

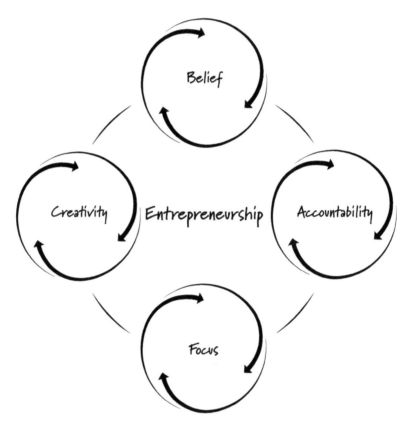

Creativity is the fourth Primary Instinct in the Cycle of Entrepreneurship

FIRST STEPS OF THE ENTREPRENEURIAL JOURNEY

If you enjoy the outdoors, you have likely hiked a trail and stopped along the way to enjoy a scenic view. The hike didn't end because you paused. Pausing and enjoying a moment of awe is part of what makes any journey rewarding. If your hike was up a mile-high mountain, pausing is important because it gives you time to reflect and regroup. It is easy to start again because you enjoy each small step along the way.

The mountain might look imposing from a distance, but those small steps make climbing it downright enjoyable. You might not have planned to make the summit. However, if you gained just half an inch of elevation with each step, you would be at the top after twenty-three miles of hiking.

The journey to self-employment might look like a mile-high mountain that is impossible to climb but only from a distance. Once you are on the trail, each small step is not terribly difficult. That is the beauty and magic of taking small steps. Over time, you imperceptibly rise and start to believe in your ability to make it to the top.

You will only believe after you start doing things differently, after you consistently take small steps.

Remember, the age-old adage that belief drives action is only true if you already believe. For everyone else, beliefs are reverse engineered. You will only believe after you start doing things differently, after you consistently take small steps. So, action comes first and starts a domino effect. Tipping over that first domino doesn't take much effort, but change is a force multiplier. The second domino falls, the third, and so on. With one small step, a cascade of events occurs. Once the cycle has started, it flows with its own momentum. It begins and ends with one small action. Take that first step, and the rest of the dominoes fall.

THE FUTURE OF ENTREPRENEURSHIP

Based on the current trajectory, 99% of the American workforce will work for the other 1% sometime in the mid-2040s. Everyone is familiar with the 1% when talking about wealth distribution and income, but what about legacy creation? What about the innate human desire to explore our limits and build something that lasts long after we are gone? What about our inner calling? If we allow just one in ten of us to experience the fulfillment and self-actualization that comes with entrepreneurship, we are sacrificing our potential on the altar of certainty.

Thousands of generations brought us to this point. Millions of our ancestors fought so that we could live free from any determination of our will and achieve everything within our innate ability. We don't just have the opportunity to explore our limits; we have an obligation to do so.

Each of us feels a connection to our lineage and the places that make us who we are. But we have forgotten *what* we are and what we were before those places ever existed. Class division and social hierarchies are not biological. They are conjured by society. They exist only because we participate in the system that created them. We believe in them because we no longer believe in ourselves.

Our Creator gave us an inner calling and balanced our adventurous spirit with an opposing force. Our success as a species required both. Together, they are our yin and yang, our fire and ice. But we have allowed one to conquer the other. The ice of uncertainty has smothered the fire of our optimism.

For the self-employment percentage in America to reach its historic highs, more than 25 million employees would have to become entrepreneurs. Based on current averages, that would create 80 million jobs and generate 20 trillion in economic output—an amount just short of our national debt. If that happened, the effects on our society would be immeasurable.

Increased entrepreneurship would yield greater health, happiness, civic engagement, and charity while lowering crime, depression, stress, and disease. Small businesses have the same positive effect on society as social services. But unlike social services, small businesses are not funded by taxpayer dollars. It's counterintuitive to say, but if you want to help your community, start by helping yourself. That is how it starts. That is how our nation gets better. That is what topples the first domino. It takes only one entrepreneur to start the chain reaction.

One small business might not sound like much, but its impact ripples through society and through time. The cycle of entrepreneurship overflows into families, charities, churches, and schools, empowering the less fortunate and future generations. Sons and daughters of entrepreneurs are significantly more likely to be business owners themselves. From one generation to the next, self-reliance weaves itself into the fabric of our society and strengthens us. It transforms communities. Entrepreneurship shaped America.

The U.S. was built upon the rejection of monarchy and a refusal to have our lives determined by those in power. People from all over the world gathered what they could carry and sailed beyond the horizon. They didn't risk everything to travel to a land of *certainty*. They believed that a better future existed across the ocean in the land of *opportunity*.

If those who founded America had been willing to submit to economic subservience, the country might not exist today. The speed of our unprecedented rise as a nation wasn't due to technological or economic advantages. Those were mere by-products of the real driver of American ingenuity—our entrepreneurial spirit. Immigrants didn't flood Ellis Island in hopes of finding a stable and predictable job. They came here to live the *real* American Dream. We, as a nation, should thank our forefathers who refused to live a life of mediocrity and for maintaining the fire of our optimism. Our country only exists because our ancestors refused to take a place in the spinning cogs of an empire.

We now find ourselves at a pivotal moment in our nation's history. We are becoming victims of our success. As more and more of us seek certainty at all costs, some who sleep under the blanket of freedom question how that fabric is woven. They want to trade our individual liberties and our right to pursue happiness for the certainty of a meager existence. They want to give control back to the tyranny that we fought to take it from. That won't require a revolution. Given the current trajectory of entrepreneurship in America, that will require only that we do nothing at all.

America has suffered through forty-seven economic recessions in its history and fought in thirteen major wars. The U.S. has seen its share of hardship. Each time, American entrepreneurs have answered the call. Whether it's steel factories manufacturing weapons or car assembly lines creating ventilators, the government and the world always turn to American entrepreneurs to save humanity. Now, it's time for aspiring entrepreneurs to save themselves.

The blanket of freedom that we all sleep under is warm and comfortable. One might say that there is no real need to leave a steady job and take even a measured risk. But there was no need for us to leave our caves, no need for us to farm the earth, no need for us to create this modern society. The world we live in didn't even exist for more than 99% of our existence. But, at some point in human history, one of our ancestors took a hard, right turn. She could have accepted a life of mediocrity and stayed in her cave. She could have raised her kids there. But she didn't, so here we are.

We now view the world through the lens of our self-proclaimed superiority, which gives us a strange kind of leverage against the accumulated weight of all that came before us. We foolishly believe that our current existence is the apex of humanity. But we perch atop our artificial definition of greatness and, therefore, think of ourselves as the owners of this world. But in reality, it's the other way around.

Throughout our history, Mother Nature has owned us. She molded and shaped us with challenges. Each time, one of our ancestors met that challenge and overcame it. In this way, she instilled in our brains the exact instincts we needed to succeed. Everything that we are, everything that we have ever achieved, has resulted from our beliefs, accountability, focus, and creativity. On land and at sea, on mountains and Mars, the spirit of entrepreneurship has overcome it all.

The precipitous decline of American entrepreneurialism is enigmatic, to say the least. The entrepreneurship gap grows every year despite our overwhelming desire for self-employment. The irony of it all is that we have risen to the challenge each time humanity has been called upon. Each time the world needs individual effort, we step up.

Now, you must step up. You must choose sides in the ancient battle between optimism and uncertainty. That decision will determine if your fate is to be part of someone else's legacy or if you will create your own.

You can choose optimism and recapture the spirit of American entrepreneurialism. Or you can ignore your instincts and succumb to the need for certainty. You must decide, and that decision will determine the future of entrepreneurship.

Personally, I am optimistic that we will rise to meet this challenge. Because if history has taught us anything, it's this: our entrepreneurial spirit will always prevail. Nothing could be more certain.

ABOUT THE AUTHOR

Tra Williams is a speaker, author, business owner, and nationally recognized expert in entrepreneurship and small business strategy. He is on a mission to rescue 1 million entrepreneurs from traditional employment. Tra has sat at the helm of two international brands and has supported thousands of entrepreneurs on their journey to self-employment. When he is not on the road empowering aspiring entrepreneurs, Tra lives and works out of his home office in sunny Florida.

(1) ask for ID b/4 surgery

mom asks R u changing your mind

do wound care outpatient
implant / infusion

(2) Kang / be cares
med regime

wound already
called serial debrivements

make incision depends on
directly over what you see
wound when you go in

extend it down - one wash

wash it well

I dont even - 2-3 days
know if we - wash close
will then rambees
be
able close it
to
maybe I'll let it heal

or might be able
suer

CPSIA information can be obtained
at www.ICGtesting.com
Printed in the USA
JSHW021408280821
18262JS00001B/1

9 781620 068717